THE NEW MERMAIDS

The Revenger's Tragedy

THE NEW MERMAIDS

General Editors
Philip Brockbank
Brian Morris

The Revenger's Tragedy

CYRIL TOURNEUR

Edited by BRIAN GIBBONS
Lecturer in English, York University

A New Mermaid

A MERMAID DRAMABOOK
HILL AND WANG • NEW YORK

Library of Congress catalog card number: 67-22729
First American Edition September 1967

Manufactured in the United States of America
234567890

For
Laurence Jagger

CONTENTS

ACKNOWLEDGEMENTS

IN EDITING the text I have made much use of Allardyce Nicoll's edition (London, 1929) and of Richard Harrier's (New York, 1963) but I occasionally consulted the fourth edition of *Dodsley's Old English Plays* (London, 1875) and J. A. Symonds' Old Mermaid and G. Sālgādo's Penguin editions. The Revels Plays edition of R. A. Foakes reached me after I had completed this edition, but I am grateful to Professor Foakes for answering an earlier enquiry. I am grateful to the librarian of the Cambridge University Library for permission to use illustrations from the emblem books of Whitney, Alciati and Ripa. For answering enquiries about copies of the quarto, I am grateful to Mr Alden of the Boston Public Library, the staff of the Chapin Library, Williamstown, Carolyn Jakeman of the Houghton Library, Harvard, Mr McManaway of the Folger Shakespeare Library and Carey Bliss of the Henry E. Huntington Library. I am grateful to Mr Bernard Harris for several valuable suggestions and to Dr Brian Morris for substantial help and guidance throughout. The introduction and commentary owe much to the works acknowledged therein, and something also to the comments of Professor M. C. Bradbrook on a paper I wrote about *The Revenger's Tragedy* two years ago.

INTRODUCTION

THE AUTHOR

SINCE 1891 there has been disagreement among scholars about the authorship of *The Revenger's Tragedy*. The various attempts to show that Tourneur was not the author have dealt with the play's imagery, its themes, its verbal and episodic parallels and echoes in other plays of the time; and the currently most popular alternative to Tourneur seems to be Thomas Middleton.[1] But if we can see close affinities between the play and the satiric comedies of Middleton, it cannot be denied that it is near kin to *The Atheist's Tragedy*, which Irving Ribner declares to be Tourneur's "with absolute certainty".[2] Yet we must recall that M. C. Bradbrook observed in 1935 that Tourneur's plays "are closest to Marston's, not only in time but in temper",[3] and we may well think that John Webster's art is often highly reminiscent of Tourneur in mood and method as well.

The difficulty is that all these playwrights are interrelated, since they wrote within the decorum of satiric drama. In Jacobean drama both satiric comedy and satiric tragedy demanded a distinct dramatic decorum, and it is demonstrable that all these playwrights used the conventions of style and form demanded by the appropriate decorum, comic or tragic. It is clear then that we cannot accept as evidence of authorship merely the citation of similar passages, for they may have been conventional, or simply lifted from a published play; and similar episodes merely bear witness to the prevalence of the tendency to work within a conventional form. Nicoll's warning that "one writer may so come under the spell of another as to have his mind filled with a phantasmagoria of images and phrases"[4] seems valid still.

There are after all remarkable affinities between *The Revenger's Tragedy* and the later *Atheist's Tragedy*, and the inferior quality of the later play may reflect Tourneur's fading inspiration. Perhaps it faded as Tourneur grew away from the influence of Marston and

[1] Irving Ribner gives a basic bibliography of the claims for Middleton's authorship in his edition of *The Atheist's Tragedy* (London, 1964) pp. xix–xx.
[2] Ribner, op cit. p. xix.
[3] M. C. Bradbrook, *Themes and Conventions of Elizabethan Tragedy* (Cambridge, 1935) chapter on Tourneur.
[4] *The Works of Cyril Tourneur* ed. Allardyce Nicoll, new issue (New York, 1963) p. 20.

Middleton. In *The Revenger's Tragedy* we may see their influence quickening his imagination and sustaining his dramatic art.

The evidence for Tourneur's authorship of the play can be succinctly stated. The first attribution was made by Edward Archer in 1656 in a playlist appended to *The Old Law*. Francis Kirkman followed suit in two lists of plays published in 1661 and 1671 as appendices to *Tom Tyler and his Wife* and *Nicomede*, respectively. There are conjectures about various entries in The Stationers' Register, but there can be little doubt that George Eld's entry on October 7 1607 refers to the play and does not offer any clue as to the author. The entry reads[5]

> Twoo plaies th one called *the revengers tragedie*
> th other. *A trick to catche the old one*.

Since any other evidence must be based on more hazy conjecture than Archer's ascription—which was made, after all, fifty years after the first edition was printed—it seems reasonable to ascribe the play to Cyril Tourneur, allowing that it reveals the influence of Thomas Middleton and John Marston and even, palely, like most Jacobean satiric plays, the influence of Ben Jonson.

Cyril Tourneur, then, was born probably between 1570 and 1580; we do not know where he was educated, but his first published work was *The Transformed Metamorphosis* which appeared in 1600, a satiric poem showing the influence of John Marston. Except for the pamphlet conjecturally ascribed to him by Nicoll, *Laugh and Lie Down*, printed in 1605, nothing is known of him until the appearance of *The Revenger's Tragedy* in 1607, and his name (as I have already said) was not connected with this play until 1656. In 1609 *A Funeral Poem Upon the Death of the most Worthy and True Soldier Sir Francis Vere* was published. Tourneur spent much of his life in the service of the Cecil and Vere families, some of it on military service abroad, and Nicoll suggested he was actively involved with military affairs in the Low Countries between 1600 and 1610. J. R. Sutherland[6] cites a letter written from Nijmegen on August 14, 1614 proving that Tourneur saw action in the Low Countries and served the Vere family, as Nicoll supposed.

In 1611 appeared *The Atheist's Tragedy*, quite certainly Tourneur's work. Some months after the September entry of this play in the Stationers' Register Edward Blount entered *The Nobleman* 'by Cyrill Tourneur' on February 15, 1611/12. This play was almost certainly acted at Court on February 23 and later near Christmas 1612/13. The

[5] *A Transcript of the Registers of the Company of Stationers of London* ed. E. Arber (London, 1875–1894) Vol. III.

[6] Cited by Ribner p. xxi.

manuscript passed into the hands of Warburton and is now lost; the catalogue listing it and other plays was destroyed by Warburton's cook.[7] Nicoll prints a musical item which may derive from the Court performance of the play; it is entitled *The Nobleman.*[8] Tourneur also probably wrote the *Character of Robert Earl of Salisbury*, a member of the Cecil family who died on May 24, 1612, and his *Grief on the Death of Prince Henry* was entered in the Stationers' Register on December 25, 1612 as "by Cirill Turnour" and printed as "by Cyril Tovrnevr" early in 1613. His last written work recorded at the time was "an act of ye Arreignment of London",[9] probably *The Bellman of London*[10] which Robert Daborne told Henslowe he had passed to Tourneur to write; the play, if it was finished, has not survived. Irving Ribner notes two small poems as also probably by Tourneur, one first published in 1899 called *On the death of a child but one year old* by "Cecill Turner", the other, rather longer than the six lines on the death of a child, being eight seven-line stanzas *Of my Lady Anne Cecill The Lord Burleigh's Daughter*, signed "C. T." and first printed in 1660.[11]

Nicoll concludes his full account of Tourneur's life by noting that on December 23, 1613 he was granted forty shillings for carrying letters to Brussels, and subsequently received a pension from the United Provinces. In 1617 he was in trouble with the Privy Council in London, but the Cecil family evidently rescued him, and he set sail with Sir Edward Cecil's fleet (under the nominal command of Buckingham) on the ill-fated Cadiz expedition in October 1625. Tourneur fell ill and was put off at Kinsale from his ship *The Royal Anne*, and died there in February 1626, according to the petition from one "Mary Turner wife of Cyrill Turner late deceased" cited by Nicoll.[12]

THE PLAY

Oh do not jest thy doom (I. ii, 49)

Paradoxically, *The Revenger's Tragedy* does not lie in the main tradition of Elizabethan revenge tragedy; in fact it may be seen as the forerunner of a group of horror tragedies, breaking the pattern

[7] See W. W. Greg, "The Bakings of Betsy" *The Library* 3rd Ser., II, (1911) p. 225.

[8] Nicoll, op. cit. pp. 257–258.

[9] ibid p. 28.

[10] Greg's conjecture.

[11] Ribner, pp. xxii–xxiii.

[12] op. cit. p. 31.

I Richly robed Death grinning beneath a mask of youthful life.

established two decades earlier in Kyd's *Spanish Tragedy.*[13] Tourneur certainly incorporates some essential elements of Kydian tragedy, but the play's vitality springs as much from other sources in Marston, in Henry Chettle's *Tragedy of Hoffman* (1603) and in Middleton's comedy. It may be tempting to over-emphasise the significance of the comic and farcical elements in the play, but Alfred Harbage has reminded us that even Kyd employed comic methods with tragic materials and that intrigue is a characteristic element in Elizabethan tragedy.[14] Nevertheless Tourneur's use of comic method is plainly much more pervasive than Kyd's or even Shakespeare's in *Titus Andronicus*, for in *The Revenger's Tragedy* the basic method of dramatic articulation seems to belong to comic art, appealing—with the exception of a few key scenes—to the intellect rather than the moral sense and the emotions. The controlling tone and atmosphere

[13] F. T. Bowers, *Elizabethan Revenge Tragedy 1587–1642*, new issue (Gloucester, Mass., 1959) p. 138.
[14] in *Essays . . . in Honour of Hardin Craig* ed. R. Hosley (New York, 1962) p. 37.

for most of the play curbs and delimits the emotion of sublime awe and profound sympathy proper to high tragedy. F. T. Bowers acutely remarks that one suspects Tourneur would have allowed Vindice to remain the hero had he not felt the lure of an unexpected ironic climax.[15] It is arguable that Vindice's fall comes about so abruptly, and with such flippancy, that it is in fact meant to be a joke, recalling similar reversals in Middleton's comedies, where for instance Hoard, in *A Trick to Catch the Old One*, falls victim and cheerfully concludes

> Who seem most crafty prove ofttimes most fools.[16]

That these dramatists choose such subjects for their jests does, of course, indicate something of the complexity and interest of their art. We may be able to understand Tourneur's art more readily by considering first the form of the play, and then examining the way in which the tragic theme is modified and shaped into this unique tragic burlesque.

We may see the play's form most clearly by relating it to three kinds of drama then popular: Senecan revenge tragedy, "Comicall Satyre" in the style of Marston and intrigue comedy in the style of Middleton.

Firstly, Vindice desires to revenge his betrothed and also his dead father—though the latter only died of discontent. These are typical motives of the hero-revenger and to them must be added his desire to purge the society of evil. Vindice, then, is a revenger of blood who believes his motives to be pure and so retains the characteristic heroic stance.

In devising his revenge, however, Vindice resembles the hero of Marston's *Malcontent*. Vindice devises an intrigue whereby he is hired by his enemy while disguised as a malcontent; operating in this and other disguises Vindice provokes discord among his enemies so that they plot against each other. In some sequences his disguise enables him to act as a detached, satirical and didactic commentator on the folly or evil of the other characters on stage. These self-sufficient sequences usually end with the exposure or punishment of such characters. *The Revenger's Tragedy*, like *The Malcontent*, has a form loose enough to allow such sequences to develop at length, as in I, iii, II, i or IV, ii.

On the other hand the play also contains several complex intrigues which are prosecuted with an urgency, a sinewy vigour in dialogue and a witty irony that insistently recall Middleton in *Michaelmas Term* or *A Trick to Catch the Old One* (1605 and 1605–6).

[15] Bowers, op. cit. p. 134.

[16] *Works of Middleton* ed. the Rev. A. Dyce (London, 1840) vol. ii; final line of the play.

These main formative influences are in some measure present—though not with assurance—in Henry Chettle's *Tragedy of Hoffman*, the play which, it seems, offered Tourneur the most direct inspiration. For Chettle's hero is a villain who believes himself pure, who calls on heaven to show it supports him—and is answered. He is a resourceful deviser of intrigue who exults at his successes:

> Trickes, and devices! longings! well 'tis good:
> Ile swim to my desires, through seas of blood.[17]

He glories in the extreme cruelty of his revenge, and contrives a series of macabre, even gruesome scenes. An example of this is the murder of Otho, who is killed by a red-hot crown clamped to his head. As he dies Otho cries out

> I feel an Aetna burne
> Within my braines, and all my body else
> Is like a hill of Ice . . .
> My sinewes shrinke like leaves parcht with the sunne
> My blood dissolves, nerves and tendons faile. (I. i)

When we turn to *The Revenger's Tragedy* itself we may be struck by the alternation between energetic, high-spirited action and brooding, slow-paced scenes of meditation on death, revenge and evil. This disturbing duality, reflected in the images of grinning skull and capering skeleton, derives partly from the medieval tradition of meditation on death, sin, and the contemptible foulness of the world, partly from a Classical and literary tradition of satire; the first profoundly personal in approach, the second essentially detached and witty.[18] There is a corresponding alternation of pace and mood in Vindice himself, now the high-spirited witty deviser of schemes, now the anguished and melancholy mourner, "still sighing o'er Death's vizard". Vindice's abrupt shifts, from his usual pose of witty superiority and immunity, to tragic involvement, indicate his change of *roles*—from satirist to tragic protagonist. There is a consequent change in Tourneur's dramatic method. This may be seen much more clearly by referring directly to the play, and I would like to illustrate from the opening scenes. What is clear above all is that Tourneur's dramatic method subordinates character and incident to his main concern, the presentation of a deeply ironic and disquieting view of human nature. For such purposes a deliberately stylised and mannered technique was fundamentally necessary.

[17] Henry Chettle, *The Tragedy of Hoffman* ed. H. Jenkins (Oxford, 1961) V. ii.

[18] For a fuller account of the distinction between Complaint and Satire see J. Peter, *Complaint and Satire in Early English Literature* (Oxford, 1956).

II Death in the costume of Folly leading away a Queen in the midst of riches and life.

III Souls damned for Avarice stamped down into Hell's cauldrons by devils.

The play opens with Vindice acting as a satiric Presenter of the dumb show unwittingly furnished by the Duke, Duchess and followers sweeping by in a blaze of torchlight. Vindice etches their several characters in harsh terms, recalling the manner of Theophrastus and the verse satirists,[19] and his soliloquy illustrates clearly his habitual tendency to swing violently from gloom to gaiety. After a sustained bitter meditation on his lost love, made the more impressive by the visual effect—a black clad figure gazing on a skull by dim torchlight—Vindice's gaiety erupts at the thought of his revenge,

[19] See for example Jonson's sketches of the characters prefixed to *Every Man Out Of His Humour* and John Donne's *Satires* I–IV.

IV God's all-seeing eye and the vainly hiding sinner. cf. Vindice's reference to

. . . that eternal eye
That sees through flesh and all

and his mind sharply visualises Revenge leading in the grinning, dancing skeletons to thrust his enemies into the cauldron of hell fire;[20] and, while this gleeful mood persists, his brother joins him.

The conversation between the brothers proceeds at the brisk pace to be expected from two witty and educated young nobles, and the spare, active verse drives their planning on:

VINDICE
Brother I'll be that strange composèd fellow.
HIPPOLITO
And I'll prefer you brother.
VINDICE Go to then,
The small'st advantage fattens wrongèd men.
It may point out Occasion; (I. i, 95–98)

When they are joined by their mother and sister the playful wit combat is replaced by a less open and assured tone; Vindice's hint of suspicion (never followed up, incidentally) about his father's death recalls Hamlet's:

[20] See Plates II and III.

V The figure Occasion; the forelock is plainly visible.

VINDICE
. . . surely I think he died
Of discontent, the nobleman's consumption.
GRATIANA
Most sure he did.
VINDICE Did he? 'Lack,—you know all,
(I. i, 125–127)

It is characteristic that Tourneur should reinforce the tone of uneasiness by leaving us to draw our own conclusions from the fact that Vindice speaks *aside* when conversing with his own mother. The playwright, no less than his hero, shapes incident with a tough, witty cynicism.

Indeed we have a sense of guiding, shaping purpose in Tourneur's whole articulation of the scene. The rhythm is significant. It begins in meditative stillness; the entry of a character initiates the planning of an intrigue and provokes a display of satiric wit, and the entry of further characters brings mounting complexity and speed to the action and a prevalent tone of unsentimental, curbed cynicism and precarious, sardonic comedy. It is this rhythm which governs the play as a whole.

The next scene is primarily a self-sufficient demonstration of the evil of corrupt justice, and its form is highly reminiscent of Marston's work. The opening dialogue between the Duke and Judge is wholly ironic, its dignified tone is deceptive, it has a seemingly unbroken patina. Only the implications of what is said betray the dramatist's concern to reveal how pervasive corruption mines all within, leaving the very vocabulary of justice and morality empty husks:

DUKE

. . . Who dares now whisper
That dares not then speak out . . .
. . . our closest shame.

VI The serpent concealed by the innocent flower.

1 JUDGE
Your Grace hath spoke like to your silver years
Full of confirmed gravity; for what is it to have
A flattering false insculption on a tomb (I. ii, 8–13)

The sententious condemnation merely intensifies the servility of the Judge's flattery. In fact this ironic inversion of values is the key to the whole situation in this scene. A prince is being tried for rape by corrupt judges controlled by the rapist Duke, the Duke's other sons plot to ensure a verdict of "guilty", the Duchess pleads for mercy on the grounds that the law should not have authority over princes! The situation is unfolded with didactic clarity as a sustained and thorough parody of order, and the judgement itself is presented in the fastest comic quick-fire dialogue, reaching towards a climax when a bathetic reversal snaps the tension and makes the whole sequence ridiculous. The defendant Younger Son has treated the trial as a farce from the beginning, of course, but the bastard Spurio provides the most memorably comic line just at the point of anti-climax:

1 JUDGE
Let that offender—
DUCHESS Live, and be in health.
1 JUDGE
Be on a scaffold—
DUKE Hold, hold, my lord.
SPURIO [*Aside*] Pox on't,
What makes my dad speak now? (I. ii, 80–82)

Tourneur's handling of this sequence is strongly reminiscent of Middleton in *Michaelmas Term* (1605) where the usurer Quomodo and his assistants intrigue to enmesh the young prodigal Easy; they persuade him to take a bond; he seems to assent, then draws back: the tension breaks with astringently comic bathos:

QUOMODO
Well . . . because I will not disgrace the gentleman, I'm content.
EASY
No sir, now you would, you shall not.
QUOMODO
[*Aside*] Cuds me, I'm undone! He's gone again.
SHORTYARD
The net's broke.[21]

The trial scene concluded, Tourneur changes the pace and mood: the Duchess draws Spurio the bastard aside to woo him, and though Spurio occasionally lightens the mood with a jest, the prevalence of heavily sensuous and sombre imagery and the arguments and pleas

[21] *Works of Middleton*, vol. i, p. 454.

for incestuous love make a strong contrast with the trial scene. Though the verse is compellingly supple, rich in variation and deceptively flexible, its images insist on the pervasive and unrelieved evil of the lovers: the sharp danger of knives, the cold brilliance of jewels, their lovemaking is the strife of devils or the contracting of scabs. Nor does this parody of an idyll last more than a few moments; even as he kisses her, Spurio is planning an intrigue with her and, as she leaves, his mind is plotting busily. Thus again the intrigue comedy takes over from the scene of tragic portents, and Spurio reveals himself cousin to Middleton's plotting Old Hoard, a predator with similar accent; here is Spurio:

> Stepmother I consent to thy desires,
> I love thy mischief well but I hate thee,
> And those three cubs thy sons, wishing confusion
> Death and disgrace may be their epitaphs;
> As for my brother . . .
> I'll loose my days upon him, hate all I!
> (I. ii, 191–195, 199)

and here Old Hoard:

> I'll mar your phrases, o'erturn your flatteries,
> Undo your windings policies and plots,
> Fall like a secret and dispatchful plague
> On your secured comforts![22]

It is in the next scene (I, iii) that the promise of exuberant gleeful action from Vindice, registered in his opening soliloquy, is fulfilled. His entry is vigorous indeed:

> What brother, am I far enough from myself?

and appropriately enough he invokes the spirit of impudence to give him aid; she does so, and Lord Lussurioso responds favourably to Vindice's greeting

> How dost sweet musk-cat? When shall we lie together?

Vindice offers an ominous yet striking jest, and the tone of slight uneasiness is marvellously caught by the brief catches in the dialogue's rhythm as Lussurioso is put off balance:

> LUSSURIOSO
> —of what profession?
> VINDICE
> A bone setter.
> LUSSURIOSO A bone setter!
> VINDICE A bawd my lord,
> One that sets bones together. (42–44)

[22] *Works of Middleton*, vol. ii, p. 36.

As the conversation proceeds, Vindice offers ostensible sympathy to Lussurioso and covert ridicule of him to the audience, and the comedy of the situation reaches its admirable climax in the passage of single line or half line dialogue (*stychomythia*) where each of Vindice's responses is totally ambiguous, instinct with savage aggression while seemingly sympathetic; it is a typical example of Jacobean satiric comedy:

LUSSURIOSO
. . . let thy heart to him
Be as a virgin, close.
VINDICE Oh my good lord.
LUSSURIOSO
We may laugh at that simple age within him—
VINDICE
Ha! Ha! Ha! (136–139)

It is no less typical of the conventions of satiric comedy that Vindice should conclude the scene with a soliloquy of towering invective against the degeneracy and corruptness he has witnessed; the didactic function is as significant as the comic, though the latter has more vigour and assurance.

If this analysis has served to reveal how Tourneur varies the pace and mood in Act I, and how the alternate modes of tragedy and satiric comedy are articulated, it might be interesting to try and see the whole play in this perspective and hence learn something about its claims to the title of "tragic burlesque".

In Act I, as we have seen, satiric comedy is lively and even farcical; but though its subject matter is unpleasant and disturbing, its action does not involve torture and murder. In the subsequent Acts, however, the various intrigues initiated in Act I lead to increasingly horrific action before the eyes of the spectator. The mood and the tone of the dialogue in these scenes of torture and death is strikingly indecorous: it is, in fact, the mood and tone of comedy, and the profound, serious reflections on tragic themes, though voiced, are notably absent when death takes place. No character reflects on his own motives or state of grace; Tourneur plainly found more interest in Hamlet's murder of Polonius ("I'll lug the guts into the neighbour room") than in his inability to plot and execute revenge.

The first of such scenes is Lussurioso's attempted murder of the Duke (II. iii) and Vindice looks forward to it with a gleeful anticipation which recalls comic tricksters in Middleton, or Jonson's Mosca in *Volpone*; and when the attempted murder fails through Lussurioso's discovery, Vindice's reaction is wholly light-hearted. This attempt at murder fails, but the situation is based on a series of ironic reversals and its conclusion ironically turns Lussurioso's attempt to

VII The lion killing the boar, with the vulture looking on and waiting to profit from death.

revenge his father's honour into an attempt on his honour. But II. iii merely whets our appetite, and soon enough in III. iv the Younger Son is led off to execution by mistake; he cannot see his own death as anything but comic:

> I thank you faith, good pretty wholesome counsel!
> I should look up to heaven as you said
> Whilst he behind me cozens me of my head!
> Ay, that's the trick. (69–72)

and his severed head serves as the focus of a farcical scene of mistaken identity (III. vi) with such absurd lines as

> Whose head's that, then?

and

> Villain I'll brain thee with it! (73, 77)

Act V begins, as I have remarked in the Commentary, with action and dialogue strongly reminiscent of *The Jew of Malta*; the stabbing of the corpse recalls Friar Jacomo's assault on the propped up corpse of Friar Barnadine, a double shock, mocking death and the Church. Marlowe's villain Ithamore intensifies the horror of that situation in gleeful tones:

> Ay, master, he's slain; look how his brains drop out on's nose.[23]

In *The Revenger's Tragedy* the mockery of death is effected more urbanely:

VINDICE
Sa, sa, sa, thump! [*He stabs the corpse*] There he lies!
LUSSURIOSO
Nimbly done. [*Approaches the corpse*] Ha! Oh villains, murderers,
'Tis the old duke my father!
VINDICE [*Aside*] That's a jest. (V. i, 58-60)

The last scenes of the play are indeed organised with an assured urbane skill; but there is more than a hint of comic method, comic form, and comic mood in the final scene itself. We might expect, knowing that Tourneur borrowed the idea of the masque of revengers from *The Malcontent*, that he would have carried over some of Marston's sombre seriousness also; but even here the farcical aspect remains dominant as a result of Tourneur's duplication of masques. The first masque is as it were a *mask* concealing a rival group of revengers; when the original revengers arrive, their proposed victims are already dead, and this ironic reversal precipitates a wittier reversal as the murderers turn their swords upon each other. The second masque has concealed its threat of murder from its own actors, and our intellectual satisfaction at this completed symmetry of pattern must curb and restrict tragic awe and horror at bloody spectacle. Vindice himself jests gaily with the dying Lussurioso, whispering torturing truth, turning his death rattle into a joke:

VINDICE
Now thou'lt not prate on't, 'twas Vindice murdered thee!
LUSSURIOSO
Oh.
VINDICE Murdered thy father!
LUSSURIOSO Oh.
VINDICE And I am he!
Tell nobody. [LUSSURIOSO *dies*] (V. iii, 78–80)

The valedictory words of Vindice have the lively, high-spirited tone of the successful comic trickster; it is impossible to take seriously the

[23] *Plays* (World's Classics series) Oxford, 1950, *The Jew of Malta*, IV, 183.

supposed tragic fall into sin of a character who leaves the stage with the words

> we have enough—
> I' faith we're well—our mother turned, our sister true,
> We die after a nest of dukes! Adieu. (V. iii, 124–126)

If it is true that the close of the play has the light-hearted vigour imparted to it by its hero, and the resolution of complex interwoven plots in a satisfying manner familiar from Middleton's comedies, it is no less true that the hero has real reason for his good humour: his blood revenge is achieved, and in as cruel a manner as could perhaps be imagined. It is the fact that Vindice's personal revenge is satisfied in III. v which gives scope for the working out of the various intrigues which either do not involve him at all or are additional to his main plan; but the scene of that revenge is of central importance in any discussion of the tragic aspects of the play, and it will perhaps be agreed that *The Revenger's Tragedy* has a tragic dimension, however original Tourneur's conception may be.

There are, as we saw in discussing Act I, several scenes in which characters meditate on revenge, death and evil in the earlier part of the play, though it is remarkable that their preoccupations are more generalised than we might expect—in fact they recall the reflections of medieval writers on sin and human frailty rather more readily than the self-centred thoughts of a tragic soliloquiser like Hamlet. It is in these passages, however, that Tourneur introduces a number of themes which find an intense, rich and compelling focus in the long scene where Vindice's revenge on the Duke and on the evil he represents finds fulfilment. The image groups in the first three Acts reverberate and gather meaning in a way comparable to those in *Hamlet*, and the tragic effect of III. v draws its sustaining profundity from the image patterns already established in preceding dialogue. It could be argued that the savagery of the actual murder and the harsh satiric cruelty of the vengeful brothers tends to reduce the full tragic effect, rather than add to it; but the scene is masterly because the stagecraft, the actions and the iconographic effect (the groupings and movement as we *see* them) all contribute to its rich climactic unity.

The preoccupations with death, sin and corruption which mark the meditative passages are expressed in images of food, land or flesh dissolving and putrefying. The speed and irreversibility of these processes is felt to be terrifying, and the metaphors of poison's corrosive action intensify this terror. To cuckold a husband is to lay acid on his brow:

> I'll kill him in his forehead, hate there feed— (I. ii, 107)

To ravish a woman is to consume her flesh: the Younger Son had "long lust to eat" into Antonio's "wearing" (clothing and flesh are equated as disguises for the skeleton in I. i) and finally succeeded

> And fed the ravenous vulture of his lust. (I. iv, 45)

The fusion of lust and disease is made in Spurio's cry

> Oh one incestuous kiss picks open hell (I. ii, 173)

and the idea of soft female flesh as a scab over putrefaction—a commonplace in medieval moral invective—is reiterated by Lussurioso:

> fairest women,
> Good only for their beauties, which washed off,
> No sin is uglier. (I. ii, 29–31)

Such images of disease corrupting beautiful female flesh are frequent not only in *Hamlet* but in Marston's comedies also, and the emblems and sculpture of the Renaissance period show a strong interest in the processes of decay and putrefaction.[24] Spurio's soliloquy in I. ii evokes the kinship of the appetites for food and for sexual pleasure:

> Faith if the truth were known I was begot
> After some gluttonous dinner—some stirring dish
> Was my first father; when deep healths went round
> And ladies cheeks were painted red with wine (178–181)

but the diction is itself rotting with sweet sibilants—

> In such a whispering and withdrawing hour,
> When base male bawds kept sentinel at stair-head

and the epicurean dishes seem to be, though delicious, putrescent. This gives a strikingly sinister undertone to Vindice's subsequent ironic rhapsody on

> the stirring meats
> Ready to move out of the dishes
> That e'en now quicken when they're eaten
> (II. i, 196–198)

and fuses the idea that sweetness and rottenness are synonymous, with the idea that disease lurks in beautiful flesh. Both beautiful, soft skinned women and epicurean dishes have in common the fact that when they dissolve they leave a stark and grimly durable frame of bones. Thus the metaphors and images drawn from skeleton and skull are linked thematically with those from food and diseased flesh. Since

[24] See Theodore Spencer, *Death and Elizabethan Tragedy* (Cambridge, Mass., 1936) and Plate VIII.

Tourneur had the habit of drawing on emblem art and woodcuts for some of his images, they have a sharp pictorial definition. In the case of those drawn from the Dance of Death there is a particular sharpness, due to the familiarity and frequency of illustrations of it at the time and, most important here, the fact that an actual skull is used in two key scenes of the play where it is the focus of the action and of the thematic imagery. Vindice's revenge on the Duke is to make him kiss the poisoned, painted mouth of a face once beautiful, now a naked skull. This act, which the audience watches, is the focus of the main themes of the imagery. It has a clear and exact ironic neatness, is wittily appropriate "wild justice"[25] and is savagely cruel as a form of satiric ridicule and punishment.

Once in the summerhouse, the appointed scene for his revenge, Vindice delivers in superbly supple, hurrying, suddenly pausing rhythms his famous speech on the temptation of flesh and the suddenness of sin

For the poor benefit of a bewitching minute (III. v, 74)

and it is in the discursive, vivid evocation of human weakness and infected spirit that Tourneur creates the tragic dimension for Vindice's revenge, the climax of the play.

However Vindice is not a tragic hero comparable to Hamlet, Lear, Othello or Macbeth. Vindice has no inner conflict with temptation to evil, he suffers no indecision, no storm rages in his "little world of man". He neither doubts nor hesitates, he does not develop or decrease in stature, he achieves no deep self-knowledge. The tragic destruction which we sense in *The Revenger's Tragedy* is evoked in the context of society and mankind at large; and that context is the traditional concern of satiric, not tragic, art.

As I have tried to show, the revenge of Vindice draws the profound and numinous themes of the meditative passages into an intense and terrible focus. When Hippolito stamps on the dying Duke he reminds the audience of the pictures and sculptures and narratives showing the fate of damned souls, thrust down into the cauldron of hell by grotesquely cruel devils after the skeleton dancers have torn them away from their worldly pleasures. The intensity with which Tourneur presents this terrifying experience, sustained by the superb, richly allusive and vivid imagery and the central significance of this theme to a Jacobean audience, gives us reason for describing Cyril Tourneur as a tragic dramatist, though the uniqueness of his art lies elsewhere.

[25] Francis Bacon's definition in his essay *Of Revenge*, an illuminating introduction to the complicated Elizabethan attitude to the subject.

The Revenger's Tragedy has not, before the 1966 Stratford-upon-Avon production, enjoyed a sympathetic and successful stage production. This failure in the theatre is difficult to understand, for the play's vitality is frenetic, sustained by the tension induced within it by the contrasting techniques and moods of tragedy, satiric comedy and farce. Jacobean jesting with faith and death should be more comprehensible to us, now, for we have learned the art of jesting with nuclear holocaust for theme.

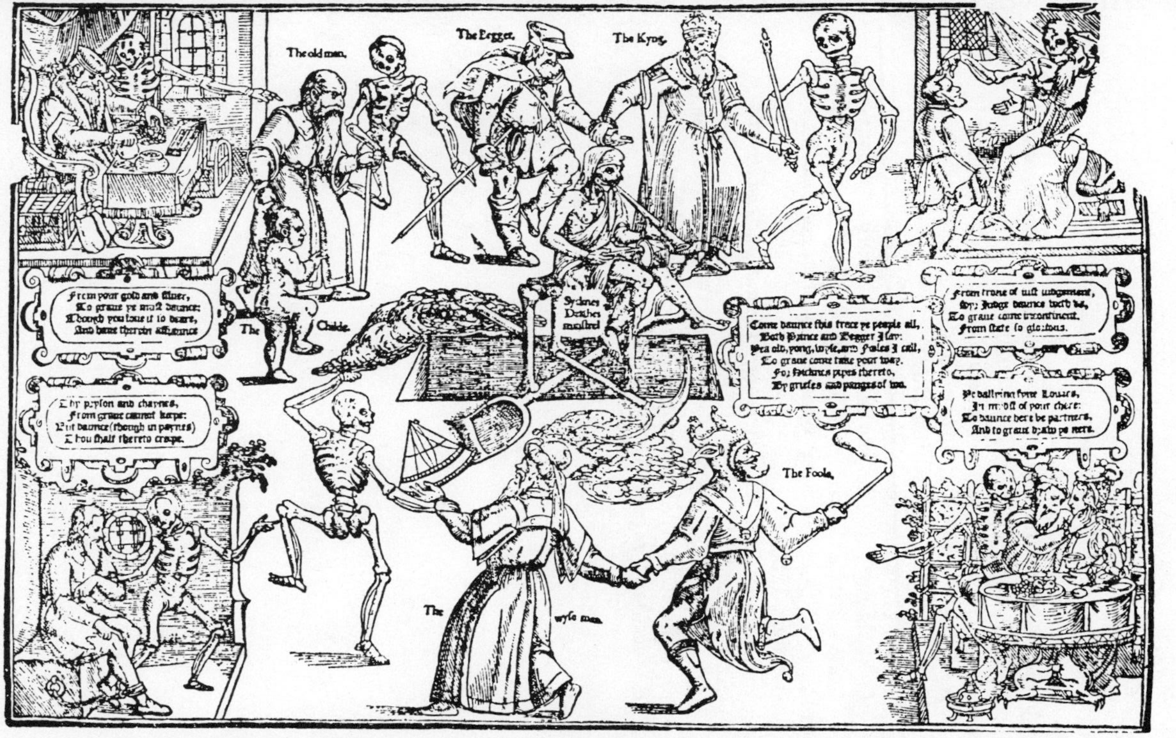

VIII Skeletons leading the Dance of Death to the tune of Sickness, Death's minstrel. The figures are the king, beggar, old man, child, wise man and fool. Other skeletons invite the rich man, the judge, the prisoner and lovers to join the dance leading to the grave in the centre of the picture. An English version.

A List of the Illustrations

THE ILLUSTRATIONS

THE EIGHT ILLUSTRATIONS have been chosen to suggest how contemporary visual art might be seen to have influenced Tourneur's dramatic imagination: they inform his poetic imagery and also his stagecraft. Thus when Vindice and Hippolito stamp on the poisoned Duke, the audience may be visually reminded of the fate of the avaricious in hell (see III); the blazing star at the beginning of Act V recalls the all-seeing eye of God, and Truth, so common in emblem art where there is an equivalent visual didactic technique (IV), while the masque in the closing moments of the play has significant associations with the Dance of Death shown in VIII. Vindice's wittiness in his *role* of revenger and moral tutor (bidding his sister and mother remember that death comes to us all) has the dramatic and sensational quality of the skeleton in the garments of Folly shown in II, especially at the death of the Duke in III. v. The remaining Plates are more indirectly relevant. VII makes the point that the cunning—though relatively puny—vulture profits from the violent death of the boar; so Vindice stands by and gleefully waits to enjoy the spectacle of angry Lussurioso's murder of his father the Duke in II. iii. The *tableau* on stage is comparable to the *tableau* in the emblem. V illustrates the close accuracy of the references in the text to Occasion, and I and VI are central images informing Tourneur's imagination. Such images are arrestingly powerful, and VI is indeed a focal image for Jacobean Tragedy as a whole; Lady Macbeth recalls it (in *Macbeth* I. v) with memorable sharpness.

NOTE ON THE TEXT

THE PLAY was first printed in 1607 by George Eld; in the following year sheets of this edition were made up and issued under a variant title page. My copy text has been the copy of the second, 1608, issue of the first edition (British Museum 644 c 80) and with it I have collated the 1607 issue (C 34 e 11) also in the British Museum. I have gathered a list of variants resulting from proof correction in the course of printing, and have added to it by consulting the editions of Allardyce Nicoll (1929) and Richard Harrier (1963). The presswork of the first printing has been analysed by George Price in an article published in Volume XV of *The Library*; it seems likely that his account is broadly satisfactory in explaining the high incidence of variants in signature H, first pointed out by Nicoll. I have aimed to reproduce the corrected text of the quarto and have allowed emendation only where manifest corruption demanded it; but I have modernised punctuation and spelling and added or amplified stage directions. The notes record all emendations and variants; square brackets enclose added or amplified stage directions and speech prefixes. Act and Scene divisions follow Harrier's edition. I have silently expanded abbreviated speech prefixes and contractions in the text. The copy text's lineation has been reproduced except where the notes record alteration.

FURTHER READING

M. C. Bradbrook, *Themes and Conventions of Elizabethan Tragedy* (Cambridge, 1935)

F. T. Bowers, *Elizabethan Revenge Tragedy 1587–1642* new issue, (Gloucester, Mass., 1959)

S. Schoenbaum, *Middleton's Tragedies* (New York, 1955)

Theodore Spencer, *Death and Elizabethan Tragedy* (Cambridge, Mass., 1936)

J. Peter, *Complaint and Satire in Early English Literature* (Oxford, 1956)

O. J. Campbell, *Comicall Satyre and Shakespeare's Troilus and Cressida* (San Marino, 1938)

Alvin Kernan, *The Cankered Muse* (New Haven, 1959)

Allardyce Nicoll, *The Works of Cyril Tourneur*, new issue (New York, 1963)

Irving Ribner's introduction to *The Atheist's Tragedy* (Revels Plays; 1964)

Peter B. Murray, *A Study of Cyril Tourneur* (Philadelphia, 1964), for an excellent bibliography.

THE REVENGERS TRAGÆDIE.

As it hath beene ſundry times Acted, by the Kings Maieſties Seruants.

AT LONDON
Printed by G. Eld, and are to be ſold at his houſe in Fleete-lane at the ſigne of the Printers-Preſſe.
1608.

[Dramatis Personae

THE DUKE
LUSSURIOSO the Duke's son
SPURIO a bastard
AMBITIOSO the Duchess' eldest son
SUPERVACUO the Duchess' second son
YOUNGER SON of the Duchess
VINDICE a revenger, also called PIATO in disguise } brothers to Castiza
HIPPOLITO also called CARLO }
ANTONIO } Nobles
PIERO }
DONDOLO
Nobles Judges Gentlemen Officers Keeper Servants
THE DUCHESS
CASTIZA
GRATIANA mother of Castiza

Scene: a city in Italy]

LUSSURIOSO meaning luxurious in the Elizabethan sense of "lecherous".
AMBITIOSO ambitious.
SUPERVACUO over-idle or foolish.
VINDICE "A revenger of wrongs . . . and abuses, one that restoreth and setteth at libertie or out of danger"—Florio, *A Worlde of Wordes* (London, 1598).
PIATO "a dish . . . a course served in at any feast" or the adjective meaning "flat", "plated" or "pleader" or "cowred down, hidden"—Florio. "Plated" seems most relevant to this play.
DONDOLO the name of a character in Marston's satiric comedy *The Fawn*; Dondolo's part is vulgar and bawdy and highly reminiscent of Marstonian comedy.
CASTIZA chastity.
GRATIANA grace.
Scene: Italy the conventional setting for satiric drama of intrigue after Marston's first plays. See G. K. Hunter, "English Folly and Italian Vice" in *Jacobean Theatre* ed. J. R. Brown and Bernard Harris (London, 1960).

The copy of Q in the Boston Public Library has a list of *dramatis personae* written in a contemporary hand on the blank verso of the title leaf; but it is hard to find this in itself evidence of use by a contemporary producer or spectator.

THE REVENGER'S TRAGEDY

Act I, Scene i

Enter VINDICE; [*then*] *the* DUKE, DUCHESS, LUSSURIOSO *her son*, SPURIO *the bastard, with a train, pass over the stage with torchlight*

VINDICE

Duke: royal lecher: go, grey haired Adultery,
And thou his son, as impious steeped as he:
And thou his bastard true-begot in evil:
And thou his duchess that will do with devil:
Four ex'lent characters!—Oh that marrowless age 5
Would stuff the hollow bones with damned desires,
And 'stead of heat kindle infernal fires
Within the spendthrift veins of a dry duke,
A parched and juiceless luxur. Oh God! one
That has scarce blood enough to live upon, 10
And he to riot it like a son and heir?
Oh the thought of that
Turns my abusèd heart-strings into fret.
Thou sallow picture of my poisoned love,
My study's ornament, thou shell of Death, 15
Once the bright face of my betrothed lady,
When life and beauty naturally filled out
These ragged imperfections;
When two heaven-pointed diamonds were set
In those unsightly rings—then 'twas a face 20

13 *fret* disharmonious sound
14 Vindice addresses a skull, the "sallow picture" of his dead mistress
20 *unsightly* unseeing and ugly

---

1 *Adultery* ed. (adultery Q). Capitalised to emphasise that the personification is not perfunctory but relates to the conventional manner of the Morality and Moral Interlude drama of the later Middle Ages. See also lines 15, 43, 50, 54.
6 *hollow bones*. A typically Marstonian preoccupation with physical decay pervades the play.
8 *dry duke*. Aged through venereal disease and semi-impotent.
11 *like a son and heir*. A commonplace simile in Jacobean satiric drama. especially that of Middleton.

So far beyond the artificial shine
Of any woman's bought complexion
That the uprightest man—if such there be,
That sin but seven times a day—broke custom
And made up eight with looking after her. 25
Oh she was able to ha' made a usurer's son
Melt all his patrimony in a kiss,
And what his father fifty years told
To have consumed, and yet his suit been cold:
But oh accursed palace! 30
Thee when thou wert apparelled in thy flesh,
The old duke poisoned,
Because thy purer part would not consent
Unto his palsey-lust; for old men lustful
Do show like young men angry—eager, violent, 35
Out-bid like their limited performances—
Oh 'ware an old man hot and vicious:
"Age as in gold, in lust is covetous."
Vengeance, thou Murder's quit-rent, and whereby
Thou show'st thyself tenant to Tragedy, 40
Oh keep thy day, hour, minute, I beseech,
For those thou hast determined. Hum, who e'er knew
Murder unpaid, faith give Revenge her due
She's kept touch hitherto—be merry, merry,
Advance thee, oh thou terror to fat folks 45
To have their costly three-piled flesh worn off
As bare as this—for banquets, ease and laughter
Can make great men, as greatness goes by clay,
But wise men, little, are more great than they.

Enter [*his*] *brother* HIPPOLITO

HIPPOLITO
Still sighing o'er Death's vizard?

22 *bought complexion* face made up with cosmetics
27 *patrimony* property or estates inherited from ancestors
28 *told* counted up
39 *quit-rent* rent paid by a freehold tenant in lieu of service to a landlord
40 *show'st* ed. (shoust Q)
44 *be merry* addressed to the imagined skeleton who grins and capers in the Dance of Death
46 *three-piled flesh* finest velvet flesh (cf. l. 31 "apparelled in thy flesh")
48–49 the quibble concerns *great* (i) large in size (ii) admirable
49 s.d. *his* ed. (her Q)

VINDICE Brother welcome, 50
What comfort bring'st thou? How go things at Court?

HIPPOLITO
In silk and silver brother: never braver.

VINDICE Puh,
Thou play'st upon my meaning, prithee say
Has that bald madam, Opportunity,
Yet thought upon's, speak, are we happy yet? 55
Thy wrongs and mine are for one scabbard fit.

HIPPOLITO
It may prove happiness?

VINDICE What is't may prove?
Give me to taste.

HIPPOLITO Give me your hearing then.
You know my place at Court.

VINDICE Ay, the duke's chamber
But 'tis a marvel thou'rt not turned out yet! 60

HIPPOLITO
Faith I have been shoved at, but 'twas still my hap
To hold by the duchess' skirt, you guess at that,
Whom such a coat keeps up can ne'er fall flat—
But to the purpose.
Last evening predecessor unto this, 65
The duke's son warily enquired for me,
Whose pleasure I attended: he began
By policy to open and unhusk me
About the time and common rumour:
But I had so much wit to keep my thoughts 70
Up in their built houses, yet afforded him
An idle satisfaction without danger,
But the whole aim and scope of his intent
Ended in this: conjuring me in private
To seek some strange digested fellow forth 75
Of ill-contented nature, either disgraced
In former times, or by new grooms displaced
Since his step-mother's nuptials: such a blood,
A man that were for evil only good;
To give you the true word some base-coined pandar. 80

VINDICE
I reach you, for I know his heat is such,
Were there as many concubines as ladies
He would not be contained, he must fly out.

54 *Opportunity* the figure usually called Occasion

I wonder how ill-featured, vile proportioned
That one should be, if she were made for woman, 85
Whom at the insurrection of his lust
He would refuse for once: heart, I think none;
Next to a skull, though more unsound than one,
Each face he meets he strongly dotes upon.

HIPPOLITO
Brother y'ave truly spoke him! 90
He knows not you, but I'll swear you know him.

VINDICE
And therefore I'll put on that knave for once,
And be a right man then, a man o' the time,
For to be honest is not to be i' the world.
Brother I'll be that strange composèd fellow. 95

HIPPOLITO
And I'll prefer you brother.

VINDICE
Go to then,
The small'st advantage fattens wrongèd men.
It may point out Occasion; if I meet her
I'll hold her by the fore-top fast enough
Or like the French mole heave up hair and all. 100
I have a habit that will fit it quaintly—
Here comes our mother.

[*Enter* GRATIANA *and* CASTIZA]

HIPPOLITO
And sister.

VINDICE
We must coin.
Women are apt you know to take false money,
But I dare stake my soul for these two creatures
Only excuse excepted, that they'll swallow 105
Because their sex is easy in belief.

GRATIANA
What news from Court son Carlo?

88 Nicoll has a full stop at the line end
92 *put on* disguise myself as 96 *prefer* recommend
96 *Go to* ed. (Go too Q) 101 *habit* costume
102 *coin* feign (with a subsequent pun on the sense "make money")
107 GRATIANA ed. (Mother Q *passim*) *Court* ed. (Cour Q)

98 *Occasion.* The emblems of the period usually show Occasion as a woman with a long forelock, standing on a turning wheel; her razor can divide armies, her flying scarf shows that she is fleet and must be seized instantly or she will escape. See Plate V.

100 *French mole.* The mole undermines a lawn as this sexual (hence "French") disease causes hair to fall out of the scalp.

HIPPOLITO Faith mother,
'Tis whispered there the duchess' youngest son
Has played a rape on Lord Antonio's wife.

GRATIANA
On that religious lady! 110

CASTIZA
Royal blood monster! He deserves to die,
If Italy had no more hopes but he.

VINDICE
Sister y'ave sentenced most direct, and true,
The Law's a woman, and would she were you.
Mother I must take leave of you. 115

GRATIANA
Leave for what?

VINDICE I intend speedy travel.

HIPPOLITO
That he does madam.

GRATIANA Speedy indeed!

VINDICE
For since my worthy father's funeral,
My life's unnatural to me, e'en compelled,
As if I lived now when I should be dead. 120

GRATIANA
Indeed he was a worthy gentleman
Had his estate been fellow to his mind.

VINDICE
The duke did much deject him.

GRATIANA Much?

VINDICE Too much.
And through disgrace oft smothered in his spirit
When it would mount, surely I think he died 125
Of discontent, the nobleman's consumption.

GRATIANA
Most sure he did.

VINDICE Did he? 'Lack,—you know all,
You were his midnight secretary.

111 *Royal blood monster!* ed. (Royall bloud: monster Q) this must refer to the Younger Son's viciousness in raping Antonio's wife; he, *not* she, has royal blood
116 *travel* ed. (travaile Q) Q's spelling may carry a pun on *travail* = hard work
119 *unnatural* ed. (unnaturally Q) 123 *Too* ed. (To Q)

118–120 The analogy with Hamlet is clear.

GRATIANA No,
He was too wise to trust me with his thoughts.

VINDICE
[*Aside*] I' faith then father thou wast wise indeed, 130
"Wives are but made to go to bed and feed".—
Come mother, sister: you'll bring me onward, brother?

HIPPOLITO
I will.

VINDICE
[*Aside*] I'll quickly turn into another. *Exeunt*

[Act I, Scene ii]

Enter the old DUKE, LUSSURIOSO *his son, the* DUCHESS, [SPURIO] *the bastard, the duchess' two sons* AMBITIOSO *and* SUPERVACUO, *the third her youngest brought out with officers for the* [*trial for*] *rape*, [*and*] *two judges*

DUKE
Duchess it is your youngest son, we're sorry,
His violent act has e'en drawn blood of honour
And stained our honours,
Thrown ink upon the forehead of our state
Which envious spirits will dip their pens into 5
After our death, and blot us in our tombs.
For that which would seem treason in our lives
Is laughter when we're dead. Who dares now whisper
That dares not then speak out, and e'en proclaim
With loud words and broad pens our closest shame. 10

1 JUDGE
Your Grace hath spoke like to your silver years
Full of confirmed gravity; for what is it to have
A flattering false insculption on a tomb
And in men's hearts reproach? The 'bowelled corpse
May be seared in, but, with free tongue I speak— 15
"The faults of great men through their sear clothes break".

DUKE
They do, we're sorry for't, it is our fate,

10 *broad pens* scurrilous writing
11 *silver years* age shown by white hair
14 *'bowelled* disembowelled to delay corruption
15 *seared* sealed
16 *sear clothes* cere cloth, waxed waterproof and used to wrap corpses
16 *sear* ed. (searce Q)

To live in fear and die to live in hate.
I leave him to your sentence: doom him, lords,
The fact is great—whilst I sit by and sigh. 20

DUCHESS
[*Kneels*] My gracious lord I pray be merciful
Although his trespass far exceed his years;
Think him to be your own as I am yours,
Call him not son in law: the law I fear
Will fall too soon upon his name and him. 25
Temper his fault with pity.

LUSSURIOSO Good my lord,
Then 'twill not taste so bitter and unpleasant
Upon the judge's palate; for offences
Gilt o'er with mercy show like fairest women,
Good only for their beauties, which washed off, 30
No sin is uglier.

AMBITIOSO I beseech your Grace,
Be soft and mild, let not relentless Law
Look with an iron forehead on our brother.

SPURIO
He yields small comfort yet—hope he shall die;
And if a bastard's wish might stand in force, 35
Would all the Court were turned into a corse.

DUCHESS
No pity yet? Must I rise fruitless then—
A wonder in a woman—are my knees
Of such low metal that without respect—

1 JUDGE
Let the offender stand forth, 40
'Tis the duke's pleasure that impartial doom
Shall take first hold of his unclean attempt.
A rape! Why 'tis the very core of lust,
Double adultery.

YOUNGER SON So sir.

2 JUDGE And which was worse,
Committed on the Lord Antonio's wife, 45

29 *Gilt o'er with mercy* the ironic effect is to imply that mercy is the devil's work
30–31 lineation adjusted from Q 30 *their* ed. (therr Q)
37 *rise fruitless* the subsequent pun is based on *rise* = swell in pregnancy
41 *doom* judgement
42 *first* Q; Dodsley in *Dodsley's Old English Plays* (1744) conjectured *fast* and R. A. Foakes follows

That general honest lady. Confess my lord:
What moved you to't?

YOUNGER SON Why flesh and blood my lord:
What should move men unto a woman else?

LUSSURIOSO
Oh do not jest thy doom, trust not an axe
Or sword too far; the Law is a wise serpent 50
And quickly can beguile thee of thy life.
Though marriage only has made thee my brother
I love thee so far: play not with thy death.

YOUNGER SON
I thank you troth, good admonitions faith,
If I'd the grace now to make use of them. 55

1 JUDGE
That lady's name has spread such a fair wing
Over all Italy that if our tongues
Were sparing toward the fact, judgement itself
Would be condemned and suffer in men's thoughts.

YOUNGER SON
Well then 'tis done, and it would please me well 60
Were it to do again. Sure she's a goddess
For I'd no power to see her and to live;
It falls out true in this for I must die.
Her beauty was ordained to be my scaffold,
And yet methinks I might be easier ceas'd; 65
My fault being sport, let me but die in jest.

1 JUDGE
This be the sentence—

DUCHESS
Oh keep't upon your tongue, let it not slip,
Death too soon steals out of a lawyer's lip,
Be not so cruel-wise.

1 JUDGE Your Grace must pardon us, 70
'Tis but the justice of the Law.

DUCHESS The Law
Is grown more subtle than a woman should be.

SPURIO
[*Aside*] Now, now he dies, rid 'em away.

DUCHESS
[*Aside*] Oh what it is to have an old-cool duke

65 *methinks* ed. (mythinks Q)
ceas'd ed. (ceast Q) Dodsley conjectures *'sess'd* and Symonds follows him

65 *ceas'd* prevented from further acts of lechery

To be as slack in tongue as in performance. 75

1 JUDGE
Confirmed, this be the doom irrevocable.

DUCHESS
Oh!

1 JUDGE Tomorrow early—

DUCHESS Pray be abed my lord.

1 JUDGE
Your Grace much wrongs yourself.

AMBITIOSO No 'tis that tongue,
Your too much right does do us too much wrong.

1 JUDGE
Let that offender—

DUCHESS Live, and be in health. 80

1 JUDGE
Be on a scaffold—

DUKE Hold, hold, my lord.

SPURIO [*Aside*] Pox on't,
What makes my dad speak now?

DUKE
We will defer the judgement till next sitting,
In the meantime let him be kept close prisoner:
Guard bear him hence.

AMBITIOSO [*Aside*] Brother this makes for thee, 85
Fear not, we'll have a trick to set thee free.

YOUNGER SON
[*Aside*] Brother I will expect it from you both,
And in that hope I rest.

SUPERVACUO Farewell, be merry.

Exit [YOUNGER SON] *with a guard*

SPURIO
Delayed, deferred, nay then if Judgement have
Cold blood, flattery and bribes will kill it. 90

DUKE
About it then my lords with your best powers,
More serious business calls upon our hours.

Exeunt; manet DUCHESS

DUCHESS
Was't ever known step-duchess was so mild
And calm as I? Some now would plot his death
With easy doctors, those loose living men, 95

75 *performance* sexual performance
81 *Pox* ed. (Pax Q)
89–90 realigned from Q

And make his withered Grace fall to his grave
And keep church better.
Some second wife would do this, and dispatch
Her double loathèd lord at meat and sleep.
Indeed 'tis true an old man's twice a child, 100
Mine cannot speak! One of his single words
Would quite have freed my youngest dearest son
From death or durance, and have made him walk
With a bold foot upon the thorny law,
Whose prickles should bow under him; but 't 'as not: 105
And therefore wedlock faith shall be forgot.
I'll kill him in his forehead, hate there feed—
That wound is deepest though it never bleed;
And here comes he whom my heart points unto,
His bastard son, but my love's true-begot; 110
Many a wealthy letter have I sent him
Swelled up with jewels, and the timorous man
Is yet but coldly kind;

[*Enter* SPURIO]

That jewel's mine that quivers in his ear,
Mocking his master's chillness and vain fear— 115
H'as spied me now.

SPURIO Madam? Your Grace so private?
My duty on your hand.

DUCHESS
Upon my hand sir, troth I think you'd fear
To kiss my hand too if my lip stood there.

SPURIO
Witness I would not madam. [*He kisses her*]

DUCHESS 'Tis a wonder, 120
For ceremony has made many fools.
It is as easy way unto a duchess
As to a hatted dame, if her love answer,
But that by timorous honours, pale respects,
Idle degrees of fear, men make their ways 125
Hard of themselves. What have you thought of me?

SPURIO
Madam I ever think of you, in duty,
Regard and—

DUCHESS Puh, upon my love I mean.

105 *'t 'as* ed. ('tis Q) meaning 'it, one of the duke's words, has not freed him'
123 *hatted dame* women of the lower classes wore hats

SPURIO

I would 'twere love, but 't 'as a fouler name
Than lust; you are my father's wife, your Grace may guess
now 130
What I could call it.

DUCHESS Why th'art his son but falsely,
'Tis a hard question whether he begot thee.

SPURIO

I' faith 'tis true too; I'm an uncertain man
Of more uncertain woman; may be his groom
O' the stable begot me—you know I know not. 135
He could ride a horse well, a shrewd suspicion—marry!
He was wondrous tall, he had his length i' faith
For peeping over half-shut holiday windows:
Men would desire him 'light. When he was afoot
He made a goodly show under a penthouse, 140
And when he rid his hat would check the signs
And clatter barbers' basins.

DUCHESS Nay, set you a horseback once
You'll ne'er 'light off.

SPURIO Indeed I am a beggar.

DUCHESS

That's more the sign thou art great—but to our love.
Let it stand firm both in thought and mind 145
That the duke was thy father: as no doubt then
He bid fair for't, thy injury is the more;
For had he cut thee a right diamond,
Thou had'st been next set in the dukedom's ring,
When his worn self like Age's easy slave 150

129 *'t 'as* ed. ('tus Q) meaning 'it has'; Nicoll emends to *'tis*
134–138 prose in Q 136 *shrewd* ed. (shrowd Q)
149 *dukedom's* ed. (duke-doomes Q) Q's spelling may contain a pun

---

138 i.e. he was tall enough to look into houses and admire the womenfolk in their best holiday clothes (or in holiday mood); their menfolk objected.

140 *penthouse.* The projecting upper storey of a building with a sloping roof. Perhaps the idea is that women could in their turn admire him as he passed below them.

141–142 Tradesmen's signs, including the basin for barbers' shops, were suspended from brackets projecting from the wall. (Cf. *Westward Ho* I. i, 156–161.)

142–143 From the proverb, used in Jonson's *Staple of News* IV, i: "set a beggar on horseback, he'll never lin till he be a gallop". The reference to exuberant speech recurs when, in II. ii, 146, Hippolito commends Vindice's eloquence.

Had dropped out of the collet into the grave.
What wrong can equal this? Canst thou be tame
And think upon't?

SPURIO
No, mad and think upon't.

DUCHESS
Who would not be revenged of such a father,
E'en the worst way? I would thank that sin 155
That could most injure him, and be in league with it.
Oh what a grief 'tis that a man should live
But once i' the world, and then to live a bastard,
The curse o' the womb, the thief of Nature,
Begot against the seventh commandment, 160
Half damned in the conception by the justice
Of that unbribed everlasting law.

SPURIO
Oh I'd a hot backed devil to my father.

DUCHESS
Would not this mad e'en Patience, make blood rough?
Who but an eunuch would not sin, his bed 165
By one false minute disinherited?

SPURIO
Ay, there's the vengeance that my birth was wrapped in,
I'll be revenged for all: now hate begin,
I'll call foul incest but a venial sin.

DUCHESS
Cold still: in vain then must a duchess woo? 170

SPURIO
Madam I blush to say what I will do.

DUCHESS
Thence flew sweet comfort, earnest and farewell.
[*She kisses him*]

SPURIO
Oh one incestuous kiss picks open hell.

DUCHESS
Faith now old duke, my vengeance shall reach high,
I'll arm thy brow with woman's heraldry. *Exit* 175

SPURIO
Duke, thou did'st do me wrong and by thy act

151 *collet* the setting for a precious stone in a ring
156 *injure* ed. (injury Q) 167 SPURIO ed. (*Spi.* Q)

---

166 *one false minute.* M. C. Bradbrook points out the importance of this theme in her essay on Tourneur in *Themes and Conventions of Elizabethan Tragedy.*

Adultery is my nature;
Faith if the truth were known I was begot
After some gluttonous dinner—some stirring dish
Was my first father; when deep healths went round 180
And ladies cheeks were painted red with wine,
Their tongues as short and nimble as their heels
Uttering words sweet and thick; and when they rose
Were merrily disposed to fall again.
In such a whispering and withdrawing hour, 185
When base male bawds kept sentinel at stair-head
Was I stol'n softly—oh damnation met
The sin of feasts, drunken adultery.
I feel it swell me; my revenge is just,
I was begot in impudent wine and lust. 190
Stepmother I consent to thy desires,
I love thy mischief well but I hate thee,
And those three cubs thy sons, wishing confusion
Death and disgrace may be their epitaphs;
As for my brother, the duke's only son, 195
Whose birth is more beholding to report
Than mine, and yet perhaps as falsely sown
—Women must not be trusted with their own—
I'll loose my days upon him, hate all I!
Duke on thy brow I'll draw my bastardy: 200
For indeed a bastard by nature should make cuckolds
Because he is the son of a cuckold maker. *Exit*

[Act I, Scene iii]

Enter VINDICE *and* HIPPOLITO, VINDICE *in disguise to attend* LUSSURIOSO *the duke's son*

VINDICE
What brother, am I far enough from myself?

183 *rose* ed. (rise Q)
187 *met* Q; Dodsley emends to *meet* (= fitting) Symonds follows
199 *loose* Q; Nicoll suggests *lose* (= use up) but I prefer *loose* (= release a powerful force)

179–187 cf. Marston, *The Malcontent* III. ii, 24–49, especially
"When in an Italian lascivious palace, a lady guardianless,
Left to the push of all allurement . . .
Her veins fill'd high with heating delicates,
Soft rest, sweet music, amorous masquerers,
Lascivious banquets, sin itself gilt o'er".

HIPPOLITO
As if another man had been sent whole
Into the world and none wist how he came.

VINDICE
It will confirm me bold—the child o' the Court;
Let blushes dwell i' the country. Impudence, 5
Thou goddess of the palace, mistress of mistresses,
To whom the costly-perfumed people pray,
Strike thou my forehead into dauntless marble,
Mine eyes to steady sapphires; turn my visage
And if I must needs glow let me blush inward 10
That this immodest season may not spy
That scholar in my cheeks, fool bashfulness,
That maid in the old time whose flush of grace
Would never suffer her to get good clothes.
Our maids are wiser and are less ashamed— 15
Save Grace the bawd I seldom hear grace named!

HIPPOLITO
Nay brother you reach out o' the verge now—

[*Enter* LUSSURIOSO *attended by servants*]

'Sfoot, the duke's son! Settle your looks.

VINDICE
Pray let me not be doubted.

HIPPOLITO
My lord—

LUSSURIOSO Hippolito?—Be absent, leave us. 20

[*Exeunt servants*]

HIPPOLITO
My lord, after long search, wary enquiries
And politic siftings I made choice of yon fellow
Whom I guess rare for many deep employments:
This our age swims within him; and if Time

6 *mistress of mistresses* ed. (Mistrs of Mistesses Q)
17 *verge* limits of acceptable comment 17–18 realigned from Q

13 *That maid.* Truth is frequently personified as a nude in emblems of the period; nakedness signified innocence; see Panofsky, *Studies in Iconology* (New York, 1939) pp. 151 ff. and R. A. Fraser, *Shakespeare's Poetics* (London, 1962) Plate VII.

16 *Grace the bawd.* The mother's name, *Gratiana*, means "grace".

24 *Time.* Panofsky remarks that Time is represented sometimes as *Kairos*, the brief decisive moment marking a turning point in life; "this concept was illustrated by the figure vulgarly known as Opportunity". Opportunity was bald except for her forelock. (*Studies in Iconology*, p. 71.)

Had so much hair I should take him for Time, 25
He is so near kin to this present minute.

LUSSURIOSO
'Tis enough,
We thank thee: yet words are but great men's blanks;
Gold though it be dumb does utter the best thanks.
[*Gives him money*]

HIPPOLITO
Your plenteous honour—an ex'lent fellow my lord. 30

LUSSURIOSO
So, give us leave— [*Exit* HIPPOLITO]
Welcome, be not far off,
We must be better acquainted. Push, be bold
With us, thy hand:

VINDICE
With all my heart i' faith!
How dost sweet musk-cat? When shall we lie together?

LUSSURIOSO
[*Aside*] Wondrous knave! 35
Gather him into boldness: 'sfoot the slave's
Already as familiar as an ague
And shakes me at his pleasure—Friend I can
Forget myself in private, but elsewhere
I pray do you remember me. 40

VINDICE
Oh very well sir—I conster myself saucy!

LUSSURIOSO
What hast been—of what profession?

VINDICE
A bone setter.

LUSSURIOSO
A bone setter!

VINDICE
A bawd my lord,
One that sets bones together.

LUSSURIOSO
Notable bluntness!
Fit, fit for me, e'en trained up to my hand.— 45
Thou hast been scrivener to much knavery then?

28 *great men's blanks* probably a document or bill with spaces left to be filled in at leisure by the receiver
31–34 prose in Q
41 *conster* construe, i.e. "you mean to say I am saucy!"
42–44 realigned from Q

---

34 *musk-cat*. Paramour, courtesan; cf. *Every Man Out Of His Humour* II. i
He sleeps with a musk-cat every night.

VINDICE

[*Aside*] Fool to abundance sir; I have been witness
To the surrenders of a thousand virgins
And not so little;
I have seen patrimonies washed apieces, 50
Fruit fields turned into bastards,
And in a world of acres
Not so much dust due to the heir 'twas left to
As would well gravel a petition.

LUSSURIOSO

[*Aside*] Fine villain! Troth I like him wondrously, 55
He's e'en shaped for my purpose.—Then thou know'st
In the world strange lust?

VINDICE

Oh Dutch lust! Fulsome lust!
Drunken procreation, which begets so many drunkards;
Some father dreads not, gone to bed in wine,
To slide from the mother and cling the daughter-in-law; 60
Some uncles are adulterous with their nieces,
Brothers with brothers' wives—Oh hour of incest!
Any kin now next to the rim o' the sister
Is man's meat in these days, and in the morning,
When they are up and dressed and their mask on, 65
Who can perceive this, save that eternal eye
That sees through flesh and all? Well—if anything be damned
It will be twelve o'clock at night: that twelve
Will never 'scape;
It is the Judas of the hours, wherein 70
Honest salvation is betrayed to sin.

LUSSURIOSO

In troth it is too; but let this talk glide.

47 *Fool* Q; Collins in his 1878 edition conjectured *'Sfoot* and the MS may have had *Pooh*, but *fool* i.e. 'lackey' makes good sense and no authority for emendation exists
50 *patrimonies washed apieces* estates dissolved by drunken profligacy
53 *left to* ed. (left too Q)
54 i.e. sand a piece of paper to dry the ink with which a petition is written
57 *Dutch lust* "Dutch" used opprobriously for excessive, gargantuan
59–60 realigned from Q

---

51 Complex imagery involving the ideas of true inheritance declining to false (usurers) and natural fruit debased by grafting with inferior stock, as well as the obvious "fruit fields sold to pay for maintaining bastards".

It is our blood to err though hell gaped loud:
Ladies know Lucifer fell, yet still are proud!
Now sir, wert thou as secret as thou'rt subtle 75
And deeply fathomed into all estates
I would embrace thee for a near employment,
And thou should'st swell in money and be able
To make lame beggars crouch to thee.

VINDICE My lord?
Secret? I ne'er had that disease o' the mother, 80
I praise my father! Why are men made close
But to keep thoughts in best? I grant you this:
Tell but some woman a secret over night,
Your doctor may find it in the urinal i' the morning;
But, my lord—

LUSSURIOSO So, thou'rt confirmed in me 85
And thus I enter thee. [*Gives him money*]

VINDICE This Indian devil
Will quickly enter any man: but a usurer,
He prevents that by entering the devil first!

LUSSURIOSO
Attend me, I am past my depth in lust
And I must swim or drown. All my desires 90
Are levelled at a virgin not far from Court,
To whom I have conveyed by messenger
Many waxed lines full of my neatest spirit,
And jewels that were able to ravish her
Without the help of man: all which and more 95
She, foolish-chaste, sent back, the messengers
Receiving frowns for answers.

VINDICE Possible?
'Tis a rare Phoenix whoe'er she be,
If your desires be such, she so repugnant:
In troth my lord I'd be revenged and marry her. 100

LUSSURIOSO
Push; the dowry of her blood and of her fortunes

73 *loud* Q (Dodsley conjectured *wide* but there is no authority)
73 *gaped loud* yawned loudly; the couplet enforces the sententious statement
89 *depth* ed. (depht Q) 93 *waxed lines* sealed letters
93 *neatest spirit* the richest, most potent inspiration of wine (Harrier)
96 *foolish-chaste* ed. (no hyphen in Q)

---

86 *Indian devil.* Silver, mined in the Indies, where devil worship and heathenism also were supposed to prevail. Avarice is also devil worship.

Are both too mean—good enough to be bad withal.
I'm one of that number can defend
Marriage is good; yet rather keep a friend.
Give me my bed by stealth—there's true delight; 105
What breeds a loathing in't but night by night?

VINDICE
A very fine religion!

LUSSURIOSO Therefore thus:
I'll trust thee in the business of my heart
Because I see thee well experienced
In this luxurious day wherein we breathe: 110
Go thou and with a smooth enchanting tongue
Bewitch her ears and cozen her of all grace;
Enter upon the portion of her soul,
Her honour, which she calls her chastity,
And bring it into expense, for honesty 115
Is like a stock of money laid to sleep
Which, ne'er so little broke, does never keep.

VINDICE
You have given it the tang i' faith my lord;
Make known the lady to me and my brain
Shall swell with strange invention: I will move it 120
Till I expire with speaking and drop down
Without a word to save me;—but I'll work—

LUSSURIOSO
We thank thee and will raise thee; receive her name.
It is the only daughter to Madam Gratiana
The late widow.

VINDICE [*Aside*] Oh, my sister, my sister! 125

LUSSURIOSO
Why dost walk aside?

VINDICE
My lord I was thinking how I might begin,
As thus—"oh lady"—or twenty hundred devices:
Her very bodkin will put a man in.

LUSSURIOSO
Ay, or the wagging of her hair. 130

VINDICE
No, that shall put you in my lord.

104 *friend* mistress
118 *given it* ed. (gint Q)
123–125 prose in Q
129 *put a man in* provide an entry

LUSSURIOSO
Shall't? Why content: dost know the daughter then?

VINDICE
Oh ex'lent well by sight.

LUSSURIOSO
That was her brother
That did prefer thee to us.

VINDICE
My lord I think so,
I knew I had seen him somewhere. 135

LUSSURIOSO
And therefore prithee let thy heart to him
Be as a virgin, close.

VINDICE
Oh my good lord.

LUSSURIOSO
We may laugh at that simple age within him—

VINDICE
Ha! Ha! Ha!

LUSSURIOSO
Himself being made the subtle instrument 140
To wind up a good fellow.

VINDICE
That's I my lord.

LUSSURIOSO
That's thou.
To entice and work his sister.

VINDICE
A pure novice!

LUSSURIOSO
'Twas finely managed.

VINDICE
Gallantly carried: a pretty-perfumed villain! 145

LUSSURIOSO
I've bethought me.
If she prove chaste still and immoveable,
Venture upon the mother, and with gifts
As I will furnish thee, begin with her.

VINDICE
Oh fie, fie, that's the wrong end my lord. 150
'Tis mere impossible that a mother by any gifts
Should become a bawd to her own daughter!

LUSSURIOSO
Nay then I see thou'rt but a puny

137 *Oh my good* ed. (Oh me good Q)
141 *wind up a good fellow* serve a thief (Nicoll)

---

152 This is what happens in Machiavelli's comedy *Mandragola* (see *The Classic Theatre* Vol. I edited by Eric Bentley, New York, 1958).

In the subtle mystery of a woman:
Why 'tis held now no dainty dish: the name 155
Is so in league with age that nowadays
It does eclipse three quarters of a mother.

VINDICE
Does it so my lord?
Let me alone then to eclipse the fourth.

LUSSURIOSO
Why well said; come I'll furnish thee: but first 160
Swear to be true in all.

VINDICE
True?

LUSSURIOSO
Nay but swear!

VINDICE
Swear? I hope your honour little doubts my faith.

LUSSURIOSO
Yet, for my humour's sake, 'cause I love swearing—

VINDICE
'Cause you love swearing, 'slud I will.

LUSSURIOSO
Why enough: 165
Ere long look to be made of better stuff.

VINDICE
That will do well indeed my lord.

LUSSURIOSO
Attend me. [*Exit*]

VINDICE
Oh,
Now let me burst, I've eaten noble poison! 170
We are made strange fellows, brother, innocent villains:
Wilt not be angry when thou hear'st on't, think'st thou?
I' faith thou shalt. Swear me to foul my sister!
Sword I durst make a promise of him to thee,
Thou shalt dis-heir him, it shall be thine honour; 175
And yet, now angry froth is down in me,
It would not prove the meanest policy
In this disguise to try the faith of both;
Another might have had the self-same office,
Some slave that would have wrought effectually, 180
Ay and perhaps o'erwrought 'em: therefore I,
Being thought travelled, will apply myself

150–155 prose in Q
158 *Does it* ed. (Dost Q)
182 *travelled* with a supplementary meaning "experienced in evil"

Unto the self-same form, forget my nature,
As if no part about me were kin to 'em,
So touch 'em—though I durst almost for good 185
Venture my lands in heaven upon their blood. *Exit*

[Act I, Scene iv]

Enter the discontented lord ANTONIO (*whose wife the duchess' youngest son ravished*)*; he discovering* [*her dead body*] *to certain lords and* [*to* PIERO *and*] HIPPOLITO

ANTONIO
Draw nearer lords and be sad witnesses
Of a fair comely building newly fallen,
Being falsely undermined. Violent rape
Has played a glorious act: behold my lords
A sight that strikes man out of me. 5

PIERO
That virtuous lady!

ANTONIO Precedent for wives!

HIPPOLITO
The blush of many women, whose chaste presence
Would e'en call shame up to their cheeks
And make pale wanton sinners have good colours—

ANTONIO
Dead! 10
Her honour first drank poison, and her life,
Being fellows in one house, did pledge her honour.

PIERO
Oh grief of many!

ANTONIO I marked not this before:
A prayer book the pillow to her cheek;
This was her rich confection, and another 15
Placed in her right hand with a leaf tucked up,
Pointing to these words:

185 *touch* test
186 *blood* ed. (good Q) Dodsley's emendation followed by all editors except Nicoll
s.d. reads in Q *discovering the body of her dead to certain lords: and Hippolito*
6 *Precedent* ed. (President Q)
11 *drank* ed. (drunke Q)

---

14 The emblematic function of the *tableau* is emphasised by Antonio.

Melius virtute mori, quam per dedecus vivere.
True and effectual it is indeed.

HIPPOLITO

My lord since you invite us to your sorrows 20
Let's truly taste 'em, that with equal comfort
As to ourselves we may relieve your wrongs:
We have grief too that yet walks without tongue:
Curae leves loquuntur, majores stupent.

ANTONIO

You deal with truth my lord. 25
Lend me but your attentions and I'll cut
Long grief into short words: last revelling night,
When torchlight made an artificial noon
About the Court, some courtiers in the mask,
Putting on better faces than their own, 30
Being full of fraud and flattery, amongst whom
The duchess' youngest son—that moth to honour—
Filled up a room; and with long lust to eat
Into my wearing, amongst all the ladies
Singled out that dear form, who ever lived 35
As cold in lust as she is now in death—
Which that step-duchess' monster knew too well—
And therefore in the height of all the revels,
When music was heard loudest, courtiers busiest,
And ladies great with laughter—Oh vicious minute! 40
Unfit, but for relation, to be spoke of—
Then with a face more impudent than his vizard
He harried her amidst a throng of pandars
That live upon damnation of both kinds
And fed the ravenous vulture of his lust. 45
Oh death to think on't! She, her honour forced,
Deemed it a nobler dowry for her name
To die with poison than to live with shame.

18 "Better die virtuous than live dishonoured"
24 "Light cares find tongue, greater cares do not" from Seneca's *Hippolitus* (Nicoll)
29 *mask* Q; Dodsley and Symonds use the spelling *masque* but Tourneur probably intended some ambiguity
32 *moth to honour* one who eats away honour
34 *wearing* the image of clothing stands for Antonio's secure and happy life
34 *wearing* Q; Dodsley emends to *warren* and Symonds follows
37 *step-duchess' monster* ed. (step Duchess-Monster Q)
39 *heard* ed. (hard Q)
41 *for relation* "the necessity of informing you"

HIPPOLITO
A wondrous lady of rare fire compact,
She's made her name an empress by that act. 50

PIERO
My lord what judgement follows the offender?

ANTONIO
Faith none my lord, it cools and is deferred.

PIERO
Delay the doom for rape?

ANTONIO
Oh you must note who 'tis should die—
The duchess' son. She'll look to be a saver: 55
"Judgement in this age is near kin to favour".

HIPPOLITO
Nay then, step forth thou bribeless officer; [*Draws sword*]
I bind you all in steel to bind you surely,
Here let your oaths meet, to be kept and paid
Which else will stick like rust and shame the blade; 60
Strengthen my vow, that if at the next sitting
Judgement speak all in gold and spare the blood
Of such a serpent, e'en before their seats
To let his soul out, which long since was found
Guilty in heaven.

ALL
We swear it and will act it. 65

ANTONIO
Kind gentlemen I thank you in mine ire.

HIPPOLITO
'Twere pity
The ruins of so fair a monument
Should not be dipped in the defacer's blood.

PIERO
Her funeral shall be wealthy, for her name 70
Merits a tomb of pearl. My lord Antonio
For this time wipe your lady from your eyes;
No doubt our grief and yours may one day court it
When we are more familiar with Revenge.

50 *empress* there may be a pun on "impress" = emblem or symbol
56 *near* ed. (nere Q)
69 *Should* ed. (Sould Q)

---

59 Recalling *Hamlet* I, v.
68 The metaphor from building, echoing that in the opening lines of the scene, is also noticeable in *The Atheist's Tragedy*.

ANTONIO

That is my comfort gentlemen, and I joy 75
In this one happiness above the rest,
Which will be called a miracle at last,
That being an old man I'd a wife so chaste. *Exeunt*

Act II, Scene i

Enter CASTIZA *the sister*

CASTIZA

How hardly shall that maiden be beset
Whose only fortunes are her constant thoughts,
That has no other child's-part but her honour
That keeps her low and empty in estate.
Maids and their honours are like poor beginners: 5
Were not sin rich there would be fewer sinners:
Why had not virtue a revenue? Well,
I know the cause: 'twould have impoverished hell.

[*Enter* DONDOLO]

How now Dondolo.

DONDOLO

Madonna, there is one as they say a thing of flesh and blood, 10
a man I take him, by his beard, that would very desirously
mouth to mouth with you.

CASTIZA

What's that?

DONDOLO

Show his teeth in your company.

CASTIZA

I understand thee not. 15

DONDOLO

Why, speak with you Madonna.

CASTIZA

Why, say so madman and cut off a great deal of dirty way.
Had it not been better spoke, in ordinary words, that one
would speak with me?

77 *miracle* ed. (miralce Q) 3 *child's-part* inheritance
10 *Madonna* ed. (Madona Q)
17–19 Harrier realigns as verse and Sālgādo follows

10–22 Dondolo's vulgar and bawdy speeches recall similar passages in Marston's comedies.

DONDOLO
Ha, ha, that's as ordinary as two shillings; I would strive a little to show myself in my place. A gentleman-usher scorns to use the phrase and fancy of a servingman. 20

CASTIZA
Yours be your own sir; go direct him hither.
[*Exit* DONDOLO]
I hope some happy tidings from my brother
That lately travelled, whom my soul affects. 25
Here he comes.

Enter VINDICE *her brother disguised*

VINDICE
Lady the best of wishes to your sex:
Fair skins and new gowns. [*Gives her a letter*]

CASTIZA Oh they shall thank you sir—
Whence this?

VINDICE Oh from a dear and worthy friend,
Mighty!

CASTIZA From whom?

VINDICE The duke's son.

CASTIZA Receive that! 30
A box o' the ear to [VINDICE] *her brother*
I swore I'd put anger in my hand
And pass the virgin limits of myself
To him that next appeared in that base office,
To be his sin's attorney. Bear to him
That figure of my hate upon thy cheek 35
Whilst 'tis yet hot, and I'll reward thee for't;
Tell him my honour shall have a rich name
When several harlots shall share his with shame:
Farewell, commend me to him in my hate! *Exit*

VINDICE
It is the sweetest box that e'er my nose came nigh: 40
The finest drawn-work cuff that e'er was worn:
I'll love this blow forever, and this cheek
Shall still henceforward take the wall of this.
Oh I'm above my tongue! Most constant sister,
In this thou hast right honourable shown; 45

21 *gentleman-usher* one of gentle rank acting as usher to one of higher rank
23 *your own* ed. (your one Q)
25 *travelled* ed. (travayld Q)
43 *take the wall* take precedence over

Many are called by their honour that have none,
Thou art approved forever in my thoughts.
It is not in the power of words to taint thee,
And yet for the salvation of my oath,
As my resolve in that point, I will lay 50
Hard siege unto my mother, though I know
A siren's tongue could not bewitch her so.

[*Enter* GRATIANA]

Mass, fitly, here she comes: thanks my disguise:
Madam good afternoon.

GRATIANA
Y'are welcome sir.

VINDICE
The next of Italy commends him to you: 55
Our mighty expectation, the duke's son.

GRATIANA
I think myself much honoured that he pleases
To rank me in his thoughts.

VINDICE
So may you lady:
One that is like to be our sudden duke—
The crown gapes for him every tide—and then 60
Commander o'er us all; do but think on him,
How blest were they now that could pleasure him,
E'en with anything almost.

GRATIANA
Ay, save their honour.

VINDICE
Tut, one would let a little of that go too
And ne'er be seen in't: ne'er be seen in't, mark you. 65
I'd wink and let it go—

GRATIANA
Marry but I would not.

VINDICE
Marry but I would I hope; I know you would too
If you'd that blood now which you gave your daughter;
To her indeed 'tis, this wheel comes about;
That man that must be all this perhaps ere morning 70
—For his white father does but mould away—
Has long desired your daughter.

GRATIANA
Desired?

VINDICE
Nay but hear me:
He desires now that will command hereafter,

55 *next of Italy* next in succession to the Duke
65 *seen in't* ed. (seen it Q)

Therefore be wise; I speak as more a friend 75
To you than him. Madam I know y'are poor,
And 'lack the day,
There are too many poor ladies already;
Why should you vex the number? 'Tis despised.
Live wealthy, rightly understand the world 80
And chide away that foolish country girl
Keeps company with your daughter, chastity.

GRATIANA

Oh fie, fie, the riches of the world cannot hire
A mother to such a most unnatural task.

VINDICE

No, but a thousand angels can. 85
Men have no power, angels must work you to it,
The world descends into such base born evils
That forty angels can make four score devils.
There will be fools still I perceive, still fools.
Would I be poor, dejected, scorned of greatness, 90
Swept from the palace, and see other daughters
Spring with the dew o'the Court, having mine own
So much desired and loved—by the duke's son!
No, I would raise my state upon her breast
And call her eyes my tenants; I would count 95
My yearly maintenance upon her cheeks,
Take coach upon her lip, and all her parts
Should keep men after men and I would ride
In pleasure upon pleasure.
You took great pains for her, once when it was, 100
Let her requite it now, though it be but some.
You brought her forth, she may well bring you home.

GRATIANA

Oh heavens, this overcomes me!

VINDICE

[*Aside*] Not, I hope, already?

GRATIANA

[*Aside*] It is too strong for me. Men know, that know us, 105
We are so weak their words can overthrow us.

77 lineation adjusted from Q
79 *vex* aggravate the problem by increasing the number
83–84 prose in Q
85 *angels* coins worth 10s.
86 *to it* ed. (too't Q)
89 *fools* ed. (foole Q)
98 *men after men* "keep me supplied with lovers"

He touched me nearly, made my virtues bate
When his tongue struck upon my poor estate.

VINDICE

[*Aside*] I e'en quake to proceed, my spirit turns edge,
I fear me she's unmothered, yet I'll venture— 110
"That woman is all male whom none can enter!"
What think you now lady, speak, are you wiser?
What said advancement to you? Thus it said:
The daughter's fall lifts up the mother's head:
Did it not madam? But I'll swear it does 115
In many places. Tut, this age fears no man—
" 'Tis no shame to be bad, because 'tis common."

GRATIANA

Ay that's the comfort on't.

VINDICE The comfort on't!
I keep the best for last; can these persuade you
To forget heaven—and— [*Gives her gold*]

GRATIANA Ay, these are they—

VINDICE Oh! 120

GRATIANA

That enchant our sex; these are the means
That govern our affections. That woman will
Not be troubled with the mother long
That sees the comfortable shine of you;
I blush to think what for your sakes I'll do. 125

VINDICE

[*Aside*] Oh suffering heaven with thy invisible finger
E'en at this instant turn the precious side
Of both mine eyeballs inward, not to see myself.

GRATIANA

Look you sir.

VINDICE Holla.

GRATIANA Let this thank your pains.

VINDICE

Oh you're a kind madam. 130

107 *bate* shrink, dwindle 121–122 lineation adjusted from Q
130 *Oh you're a kind madam* ed. (O you'r a kind Mad-man Q)

---

117 *'tis common.* cf. *Hamlet* I, ii:
Gertrude "Thou know'st 'tis common, all that lives must die
Passing through nature to eternity.
Hamlet Ay madam, it is common."
123 *the mother*. Hysteria; cf. *King Lear* II, iv
"O how this mother swells up toward my heart".

GRATIANA
I'll see how I can move.

VINDICE
Your words will sting.

GRATIANA
If she be still chaste I'll ne'er call her mine.

VINDICE
[*Aside*] Spoke truer than you meant it.

GRATIANA
Daughter Castiza.

[*Enter* CASTIZA]

CASTIZA
Madam.

VINDICE
Oh she's yonder.
Meet her. Troops of celestial soldiers guard her heart: 135
Yon dam has devils enough to take her part.

CASTIZA
Madam what makes yon evil-officed man
In presence of you?

GRATIANA
Why?

CASTIZA
He lately brought
Immodest writing sent from the duke's son
To tempt me to dishonourable act. 140

GRATIANA
Dishonourable act? Good honourable fool,
That wouldst be honest 'cause thou wouldst be so,
Producing no one reason but thy will;
And 't'as a good report, prettily commended—
But pray by whom? Mean people, ignorant people! 145
The better sort I'm sure cannot abide it,
And by what rule should we square out our lives
But by our betters' actions? Oh if thou knew'st
What 'twere to lose it, thou would never keep it:
But there's a cold curse laid upon all maids, 150
Whilst others clip the sun they clasp the shades!
Virginity is paradise, locked up.
You cannot come by yourselves without fee,
And 'twas decreed that man should keep the key:
Deny advancement, treasure, the duke's son! 155

147 *should* ed. (shouldst Q) 151 *others* ed. (other Q)

---

135 cf. *Hamlet* I, iv
"Angels and ministers of grace defend us".

146 *The better sort*. This use of "better" indicates the confused and ambiguous moral values of Court society.

CASTIZA
I cry you mercy; lady I mistook you,
Pray did you see my mother? Which way went you?
Pray God I have not lost her.

VINDICE [*Aside*] Prettily put by.

GRATIANA
Are you as proud to me as coy to him?
Do you not know me now?

CASTIZA Why are you she? 160
The world's so changed, one shape into another,
It is a wise child now that knows her mother.

VINDICE
[*Aside*] Most right i' faith.

GRATIANA
I owe your cheek my hand
For that presumption now, but I'll forget it; 165
Come you shall leave those childish 'haviours
And understand your time; fortunes flow to you
—What, will you be a girl?
If all feared drowning that spy waves ashore
Gold would grow rich and all the merchants poor. 170

CASTIZA
It is a pretty saying of a wicked one,
But methinks now it does not show so well
Out of your mouth—better in his.

VINDICE
[*Aside*] Faith bad enough in both
Were I in earnest—as I'll seem no less.— 175
I wonder lady your own mother's words
Cannot be taken, nor stand in full force.
'Tis honesty you urge: what's honesty?
'Tis but heaven's beggar; and what woman is
So foolish to keep honesty 180
And be not able to keep herself? No,
Times are grown wiser and will keep less charge.
A maid that has small portion now intends
To break up house and live upon her friends;
How blest are you: you have happiness alone; 185
Others must fall to thousands, you to one
Sufficient in himself to make your forehead

162 alluding to the proverb
164 "I ought to slap you"
179–180 lineation adjusted from Q

Dazzle the world with jewels, and petitionary people
Start at your presence.

GRATIANA Oh if I were young
I should be ravished!

CASTIZA Ay, to lose your honour. 190

VINDICE
'Slid, how can you lose your honour
To deal with my lord's grace?
He'll add more honour to it by his title;
Your mother will tell you how.

GRATIANA That I will.

VINDICE
Oh think upon the pleasure of the palace, 195
Securèd ease and state; the stirring meats
Ready to move out of the dishes
That e'en now quicken when they're eaten;
Banquets abroad by torchlight, Musics, sports,
Bare-headed vassals that had ne'er the fortune 200
To keep on their own hats, but let horns wear 'em;
Nine coaches waiting—hurry, hurry, hurry—

CASTIZA
Ay, to the devil!

VINDICE
[*Aside*] Ay, to the devil.—To the duke by my faith!

GRATIANA
Ay, to the duke. Daughter you'd scorn to think 205
O' the devil an you were there once.

VINDICE
[*Aside*] True, for most there are as proud as he
For his heart, i' faith.—
Who'd sit at home in a neglected room

197–198 lineation adjusted from Q
198 *quicken* make you feel lively *or* come alive
199 *Musics* Q; but Dodsley, Symonds and Sālgādo read *music*. For Tourneur's usage cf. Milton's *At a Solemn Musick*
201 *horns* antlers used as hatracks; there is also a glance at the horns of cuckolds
205–208 prose in Q
206 *O' the* ed. (ath Q)
an ed. (and Q)

187–188 For a superb example of Jacobean jewellery for the forehead, see the miniature by Isaac Oliver (in the *Victoria and Albert Museum*) of a lady in masque costume: the pendent pearls set off her smooth forehead, jewels flash in her hair.

Dealing her short-lived beauty to the pictures 210
That are as useless as old men, when those
Poorer in face and fortune than herself
Walk with a hundred acres on their backs—
Fair meadows cut into green foreparts—oh,
It was the greatest blessing ever happened to women 215
When farmers' sons agreed, and met again,
To wash their hands and come up gentlemen;
The commonwealth has flourished ever since.
Lands that were meat by the rod—that labour's spared—
Tailors ride down and measure 'em by the yard. 220
Fair trees, those comely foretops of the field,
Are cut to maintain head-tires: much untold.
All thrives but Chastity, she lies a-cold.
Nay shall I come nearer to you: mark but this:
Why are there so few honest women but 225
Because 'tis the poorer profession?
That's accounted best that's best followed,
Least in trade, least in fashion,
And that's not honesty, believe it; and do
But note the low and dejected price of it: 230
"Lose but a pearl, we search and cannot brook it;
But that once gone, who is so mad to look it?"

GRATIANA
Troth he says true.

CASTIZA
False! I defy you both:
I have endured you with an ear of fire,
Your tongues have struck hot irons on my face; 235
Mother, come from that poisonous woman there.

GRATIANA
Where?

211 *useless* sexually impotent
217 *come up* i.e. to town
219 *meat by the rod* measured by the rod
221 *foretops* front lock of hair, arranged ornamentally
222 *head-tires* head dresses
223 *Chastity* Q; capitalised because a strongly realised personification
225–229 prose in Q
230 *low* ed. (loue Q)
231 *brook* find and profit by
232 *that* i.e. virginity, honesty

---

214 *green foreparts.* (i) the park in front of a manor house (ii) ornamental covering for the breast (iii) *The Atheist's Tragedy* II, v, 145 has a bawdy quibble on *fore-door* which may be present here.

CASTIZA
Do you not see her? She's too inward then:
Slave perish in thy office; you heavens please
Henceforth to make the mother a disease 240
Which first begins with me; yet I've outgone you. *Exit*

VINDICE
[*Aside*] Oh angels clap your wings upon the skies
And give this virgin crystal plaudities!

GRATIANA
Peevish, coy, foolish! But return this answer:
My lord shall be most welcome when his pleasure 245
Conducts him this way; I will sway mine own:
Women with women can work best alone. *Exit*

VINDICE
Indeed I'll tell him so.
Oh more uncivil, more unnatural
Than those base-titled creatures that look downward, 250
Why does not heaven turn black or with a frown
Undo the world? Why does not earth start up
And strike the sins that tread upon it? Oh,
Were't not for gold and women there would be no
damnation,
Hell would look like a lord's great kitchen without fire in't; 255
But 'twas decreed before the world began
That they should be the hooks to catch at man. *Exit*

[Act II, Scene ii]

Enter LUSSURIOSO *with* HIPPOLITO (VINDICE'S *brother*)

LUSSURIOSO
I much applaud
Thy judgement, thou art well read in a fellow,
And 'tis the deepest art to study man.
I know this which I never learned in schools,
The world's divided into knaves and fools. 5

HIPPOLITO
[*Aside*] Knave in your face my lord—behind your back!

243 *crystal* Q; but Q spelling *Christall* suggests subsidiary meaning "Christ-like"
251 *turn* ed. (tnrne Q)
253 *upon it* ed. (upon't Q)
1–2 prose in Q
6 "I'll call you a knave outright—behind your back!"

LUSSURIOSO
And I much thank thee that thou hast preferred
A fellow of discourse, well mingled,
And whose brain time hath seasoned.

HIPPOLITO True my lord,
We shall find season once I hope.—[*Aside*] Oh villain, 10
To make such an unnatural slave of me!—But—

[*Enter* VINDICE *disguised*]

LUSSURIOSO
Mass here he comes.

HIPPOLITO [*Aside*] And now shall I
Have free leave to depart.

LUSSURIOSO Your absence—leave us.

HIPPOLITO
[*Aside*] Are not my thoughts true? I must remove;
But brother you may stay. 15
Heart, we are both made bawds a new found way! ***Exit***

LUSSURIOSO
Now, we're an even number: a third man's
Dangerous, especially her brother.
Say, be free, have I a pleasure toward?

VINDICE Oh my lord.

LUSSURIOSO
Ravish me in thine answer: art thou rare, 20
Hast thou beguiled her of salvation
And rubbed hell o'er with honey? Is she a woman?

VINDICE
In all but in desire.

LUSSURIOSO Then she's in nothing—
I bate in courage now.

VINDICE The word I brought
Might well have made indifferent honest naught; 25
A right good woman in these days is changed
Into white money with less labour far—
Many a maid has turned to Mahomet
With easier working. I durst undertake,
Upon the pawn and forfeit of my life 30
With half those words to flat a Puritan's wife,

17–19 prose in Q
27 *white* silver
28 i.e. been persuaded to give up her Christian faith for some strange foreign religion

But she is close and good; yet 'tis a doubt
By this time—oh the mother, the mother!

LUSSURIOSO
I never thought their sex had been a wonder
Until this minute: what fruit from the mother? 35

VINDICE
[*Aside*] Now must I blister my soul, be forsworn,
Or shame the woman that received me first.
I will be true; thou liv'st not to proclaim;
Spoke to a dying man shame has no shame.
My lord.

LUSSURIOSO Who's that?

VINDICE Here's none but I my lord. 40

LUSSURIOSO
What would thy haste utter?

VINDICE Comfort.

LUSSURIOSO Welcome..

VINDICE
The maid being dull, having no mind to travel
Into unknown lands, what did me straight
But set spurs to the mother; golden spurs
Will put her to a false gallop in a trice. 45

LUSSURIOSO
Is't possible that in this
The mother should be damned before the daughter?

VINDICE
Oh that's good manners my lord: the mother for
Her age must go foremost you know.

LUSSURIOSO
Thou'st spoke that true! But where comes in this comfort? 50

VINDICE
In a fine place my lord. The unnatural mother
Did with her tongue so hard beset her honour
That the poor fool was struck to silent wonder;
Yet still the maid like an unlighted taper
Was cold and chaste, save that her mother's breath 55
Did blow fire on her cheeks. The girl departed
But the good ancient madam, half mad, threw me
These promising words which I took deeply note of:
"My lord shall be most welcome,"—

LUSSURIOSO Faith I thank her!

32–33 lineation adjusted from Q
47–49 prose in Q
56 *cheeks* ed. (checkes Q)

VINDICE
"When his pleasure conducts him this way"— 60
LUSSURIOSO
That shall be soon i' faith!
VINDICE "I will sway mine own"—
LUSSURIOSO
She does the wiser, I commend her for't.
VINDICE
"Women with women can work best alone."
LUSSURIOSO
By this light and so they can; give 'em
Their due, men are not comparable to 'em. 65
VINDICE
No that's true, for you shall have one woman
Knit more in a hour than any man
Can ravel again in seven and twenty year.
LUSSURIOSO
Now my desires are happy, I'll make 'em freemen now.
Thou art a precious fellow, faith I love thee, 70
Be wise and make it thy revenue: beg, leg!
What office couldst thou be ambitious for?
VINDICE
Office my lord? Marry if I might
Have my wish I would have one that was never begged yet.
LUSSURIOSO
Nay then thou canst have none.
VINDICE Yes my lord, 75
I could pick out another office yet,
Nay and keep a horse and drab upon it.
LUSSURIOSO
Prithee good bluntness tell me—
VINDICE
Why I would desire but this my lord:
To have all the fees behind the arras, and all 80

64–65 prose in Q
71 *beg, leg* beg and bow in a servile manner
73 Vindice's exchanges with Lussurioso in prose in Q
77 *upon it* ed. (uppont Q) 77 *drab* mistress

80 *fees*. i.e. the monopoly of all embraces behind the arras hangings and on the floor; this is a glance at the abuses in distribution of monopolies at James I's Court and the extraordinary range of commercial activities involved. A Member in one of the early Jacobean parliamentary debates on monopolies observed that bread was even likely to be monopolised!

The farthingales that fall plump about
Twelve o'clock at night upon the rushes.

LUSSURIOSO
Thou'rt a mad apprehensive knave:
Dost think to make any great purchase of that?

VINDICE
Oh 'tis an unknown thing my lord; I wonder　85
'T'as been missed so long!

LUSSURIOSO
Well this night I'll visit her, and 'tis till then
A year in my desires. Farewell, attend,
Trust me with thy preferment.　*Exit*

VINDICE　My loved lord.—
Oh shall I kill him o' the wrong-side now? No,　90
Sword thou wast never a back-biter yet.
I'll pierce him to his face, he shall die looking upon me;
Thy veins are swelled with lust, this shall unfill 'em:
Great men were gods if beggars could not kill 'em.
Forgive me heaven to call my mother wicked,　95
Oh lessen not my days upon the earth!
I cannot honour her; by this I fear me
Her tongue has turned my sister into use.
I was a villain not to be forsworn
To this our lecherous hope, the duke's son;　100
For lawyers, merchants, some divines and all,
Count beneficial perjury a sin small.
It shall go hard yet but I'll guard her honour
And keep the ports sure.

Enter HIPPOLITO

HIPPOLITO
Brother how goes the world? I would know news　105
Of you, but I have news to tell you.

83 *apprehensive* keen witted
83–86 prose in Q
98 *use* the gold of virginity made current among several men
105–106 lineation adjusted from Q

---

90 cf. *Hamlet* III, iii "Now might I do it pat".
96 Alluding to *Exodus* xx, 12 "honour thy father and thy mother: that thy days may be long" (Harrier).
102 *beneficial perjury*. Equivocation, justifiable lying in a "good" cause; the Jesuit Father Garnet was tried in 1606 for complicity in the Gunpowder Plot and was executed after admitting to equivocation; the Porter in *Macbeth* refers to the matter.

VINDICE
What, in the name of knavery?
HIPPOLITO Knavery faith:
This vicious old duke's worthily abused,
The pen of his bastard writes him cuckold!
VINDICE
His bastard?
HIPPOLITO Pray believe it; he and the duchess 110
By night meet in their linen, they have been seen
By stair-foot pandars.
VINDICE Oh sin foul and deep,
Great faults are winked at when the duke's asleep.
See, see, here comes the Spurio—

[*Enter* SPURIO *with two men*]

HIPPOLITO Monstrous luxur!
VINDICE
Unbraced: two of his valiant bawds with him. 115
Oh there's a wicked whisper; hell is in his ear.
Stay, let's observe his passage.— [*They retire*]
SPURIO
Oh but are you sure on't?
SERVANT
My lord most sure on't, for 'twas spoke by one
That is most inward with the duke's son's lust; 120
That he intends within this hour to steal
Unto Hippolito's sister, whose chaste life
The mother has corrupted for his use.
SPURIO
Sweet word, sweet occasion, faith then brother
I'll disinherit you in as short time 125
As I was when I was begot in haste,
I'll damn you at your pleasure: precious deed!
After your lust oh 'twill be fine to bleed!
Come let our passing out be soft and wary.
Exeunt [SPURIO *and two men*]
VINDICE
Mark, there, there, that step! Now to the duchess; 130
This their second meeting writes the duke cuckold
With new additions, his horns newly revived;

115 *Unbraced:* Q ending Vindice's interrupted sentence from line 114
115 *Unbraced* without his doublet
130 VINDICE ed. (*Vi.* Q)
132 *new additions* in the sense (ironic) of honours

Night, thou that look'st like funeral herald's fees
Torn down betimes i' the morning, thou hang'st fitly
To grace those sins that have no grace at all. 135
Now 'tis full sea abed over the world,
There's juggling of all sides. Some that were maids
E'en at sunset are now perhaps i' the toll-book;
This woman in immodest thin apparel
Lets in her friend by water, here a dame 140
Cunning, nails leather hinges to a door
To avoid proclamation.
Now cuckolds are a-coining, apace, apace, apace, apace!
And careful sisters spin that thread i' the night
That does maintain them and their bawds i' the day. 145

HIPPOLITO
You flow well brother.

VINDICE
Puh I'm shallow yet,
Too sparing and too modest; shall I tell thee,
If every trick were told that's dealt by night
There are few here that would not blush outright.

HIPPOLITO
I am of that belief too.

VINDICE
Who's this comes? 150

[*Enter* LUSSURIOSO]

The duke's son up so late! Brother fall back
And you shall learn some mischief.—My good lord.

133 *fees* or *phease*, hangings of black cloth put up for a funeral (Collins)
136 *full sea* high tide, climax, of excitement
138 *toll-book* deliberately incongruous: the toll-book listed horses for sale at a fair
138 *sunset* ed. (snn set Q)
i' the ed. (ith Q)
142 *proclamation* public exposure as adulteresses or whores

---

141 *leather hinges*. cf. *Malcontent* I. vii, 38–41, *Atheist's Tragedy* I. iv, 146; Ribner notes that Aristophanes mentions the use of water by Athenian ladies to silence door hinges.
150–151 Q reads as follows *Vind.* Whose this comes,
[C.W.] The [D4r]
Vind. The Dukes sonne [D4v]
Collier, Symonds, Harrier and Sālgādo assign *Whose this comes* to Hippolito; but as the catch word ignores the second speech heading, I follow Nicoll in assuming that the speech heading to line 151 is a mistake.

LUSSURIOSO
Piato, why the man I wished for, come,
I do embrace this season for the fittest
To taste of that young lady.

VINDICE [*Aside*] Heart and hell! 155

HIPPOLITO
[*Aside*] Damned villain!

VINDICE
[*Aside*] I ha' no way now to cross it, but to kill him.

LUSSURIOSO
Come, only thou and I.

VINDICE My lord, my lord.

LUSSURIOSO
Why dost thou start us?

VINDICE
I'd almost forgot—the bastard!

LUSSURIOSO What of him? 160

VINDICE
This night, this hour—this minute, now—

LUSSURIOSO
What? What?

VINDICE Shadows the duchess—

LUSSURIOSO Horrible word.

VINDICE
And like strong poison eats
Into the duke your father's forehead.

LUSSURIOSO Oh!

VINDICE
He makes horn royal.

LUSSURIOSO Most ignoble slave! 165

VINDICE
This is the fruit of two beds.

LUSSURIOSO I am mad.

VINDICE
That passage he trod warily.

LUSSURIOSO He did!

VINDICE
And hushed his villains every step he took.

153 *Piato* (i) "flat, squat, cowred down, hidden" (ii) "plated" (iii) "pleader"; these three meanings given in Florio's *A Worlde of Wordes* are discussed by Peter Murray in his study of Tourneur; it seems to me that as a name for Vindice, the second of Florio's meanings, "plated", is most appropriate.

163–164 Two thematic images fuse in this simile.

LUSSURIOSO
His villains! I'll confound them.

VINDICE
Take 'em finely, finely now. 170

LUSSURIOSO
The duchess' chamber door shall not control me.
Exeunt [LUSSURIOSO *and* VINDICE]

HIPPOLITO
Good, happy, swift, there's gunpowder i' the Court,
Wildfire at midnight! In this heedless fury
He may show violence to cross himself:
I'll follow the event. *Exit* 175

[Act II, Scene iii]

[*The* DUKE *and* DUCHESS *discovered in bed.*] *Enter again* [LUSSURIOSO *and* VINDICE *disguised*]

LUSSURIOSO
Where is that villain?

VINDICE
Softly my lord and you may take 'em twisted.

LUSSURIOSO
I care not how!

VINDICE Oh 'twill be glorious,
To kill 'em doubled, when they're heaped—be soft my lord.

LUSSURIOSO
Away! My spleen is not so lazy—thus, and thus, 5
I'll shake their eyelids ope and with my sword
Shut 'em again for ever: villain! Strumpet!
[*They approach the bed*]

DUKE
You upper guard defend us!

DUCHESS Treason, treason!

DUKE
Oh take me not in sleep, I have great sins,
I must have days, nay months dear son, with 10
Penitential heaves,
To lift 'em out and not to die unclear;
Oh thou wilt kill me both in heaven and here.

LUSSURIOSO
I am amazed to death.

8–11 lineation adjusted from Q
11 *heaves* sighs

DUKE Nay villain, traitor,
Worse than the foulest epithet, now I'll grip thee 15
E'en with the nerves of wrath, and throw thy head
Amongst the lawyers. Guard!

Enter nobles and sons [AMBITIOSO *and* SUPERVACUO *with* HIPPOLITO]

1 NOBLE
How comes the quiet of your Grace disturbed?

DUKE
This boy that should be myself after me
Would be myself before me, and in heat 20
Of that ambition bloodily rushed in
Intending to depose me in my bed.

2 NOBLE
Duty and natural loyalty forfend!

DUCHESS
He called his father villain and me strumpet,
A word that I abhor to 'file my lips with. 25

AMBITIOSO
That was not so well done brother!

LUSSURIOSO I am abused:
I know there's no excuse can do me good.

VINDICE
[*Aside to* HIPPOLITO] 'Tis now good policy to be from sight;
His vicious purpose to our sister's honour
Is crossed beyond our thought. 30

HIPPOLITO
You little dreamed his father slept here?

VINDICE
Oh 'twas far beyond me.
But since it fell so—without frightful word—
Would he had killed him, 'twould have eased our swords.
[*Exeunt* VINDICE *and* HIPPOLITO *stealthily*]

DUKE
Be comforted our duchess, he shall die. 35

LUSSURIOSO
Where's this slave-pandar now? Out of mine eye,
Guilty of this abuse.

15 *grip* ed. (gripe Q) Q spelling may indicate secondary meaning
17 *Lawyers. Guard!* ed. (lawyers gard Q)
18 *Grace* ed. (Gtace Q) 25 *'file* defile
34 s.d. [*Exeunt* VINDICE *and* HIPPOLITO *stealthily*] ed. (*dissemble a flight* Q)

Enter SPURIO *with his villains*

SPURIO
Y'are villains, fablers,
You have knaves' chins and harlots' tongues, you lie,
And I will damn you with one meal a day! 40

1 SERVANT
Oh good my lord!

SPURIO 'Sblood you shall never sup.

2 SERVANT
Oh I beseech you sir!

SPURIO To let my sword
Catch cold so long and miss him!

1 SERVANT Troth my lord,
'Twas his intent to meet there.

SPURIO Heart he's yonder!
Ha? What news here? Is the day out o' the socket, 45
That it is noon at midnight, the Court up?
How comes the guard so saucy with his elbows?

LUSSURIOSO
The bastard here?
Nay then the truth of my intent shall out—
My lord and father, hear me.

DUKE Bear him hence. 50

LUSSURIOSO
I can with loyalty excuse—

DUKE
Excuse? To prison with the villain:
Death shall not long lag after him.

SPURIO
[*Aside*] Good i' faith, then 'tis not much amiss.

LUSSURIOSO
Brothers my best release lies on your tongues, 55
I pray persuade for me.

AMBITIOSO It is our duties:
Make yourself sure of us.

SUPERVACUO We'll sweat in pleading.

LUSSURIOSO
And I may live to thank you.

Exeunt [LUSSURIOSO *and guards*]

AMBITIOSO [*Aside*] No, thy death
Shall thank me better.

SPURIO [*Aside*] He's gone—I'll after him,

56–59 lineation adjusted from Q

And know his trespass, seem to bear a part 60
In all his ills—but with a Puritan heart. *Exit*

AMBITIOSO
Now brother let our hate and love be woven
So subtly together that in speaking
One word for his life, we may make three for his death;
The craftiest pleader gets most gold for breath. 65

SUPERVACUO
Set on, I'll not be far behind you brother.

DUKE
Is't possible a son should
Be disobedient as far as the sword?
It is the highest, he can go no farther.

AMBITIOSO
My gracious lord take pity.

DUKE
Pity, boys? 70

AMBITIOSO
Nay we'd be loth to move your grace too much:
We know the trespass is unpardonable,
Black, wicked and unnatural.

SUPERVACUO
In a son, oh monstrous!

AMBITIOSO
Yet my lord
A duke's soft hand strokes the rough head of law 75
And makes it lie smooth.

DUKE
But my hand shall ne'er do't.

AMBITIOSO
That as you please my lord.

SUPERVACUO
We must needs confess
Some father would have entered into hate
So deadly pointed, that before his eyes
He would ha' seen the execution sound 80
Without corrupted favour.

AMBITIOSO
But my lord,
Your Grace may live the wonder of all times
In pard'ning that offence which never yet
Had face to beg a pardon.

DUKE
Honey how's this?

AMBITIOSO
Forgive him good my lord, he's your own son, 85
And—I must needs say—'twas the vilelier done.

61 *Puritan* hypocritical
63–64 lineation adjusted from Q 67–69 prose in Q

SUPERVACUO
He's the next heir; yet this true reason gathers;
None can possess that dispossess their fathers.
Be merciful—

DUKE [*Aside*] Here's no stepmother's wit:
I'll try 'em both upon their love and hate. 90

AMBITIOSO
Be merciful—although—

DUKE You have prevailed,
My wrath like flaming wax hath spent itself,
I know 'twas but some peevish moon in him:
Go, let him be released.

SUPERVACUO [*Aside*] 'Sfoot how now brother?

AMBITIOSO
Your Grace doth please to speak beside your spleen; 95
I would it were so happy.

DUKE Why, go release him.

SUPERVACUO
Oh my good lord I know the fault's too weighty
And full of general loathing, too inhuman,
Rather by all men's voices worthy death.

DUKE
'Tis true too. Here then receive this signet; 100
Doom shall pass. Direct it to the judges.
He shall die ere many days;—make haste.

AMBITIOSO
All speed that may be.
We could have wished his burden not so sore,
We knew your Grace did but delay before. 105

Exeunt [AMBITIOSO *and* SUPERVACUO]

DUKE
Here's envy with a poor thin cover o'er it,
Like scarlet hid in lawn, easily spied through;
This their ambition by the mother's side
Is dangerous and for safety must be purged.
I will prevent their envies, sure it was 110
But some mistaken fury in our son

93 *moon* fit of frenzy or lunacy
98 *inhuman* ed. (inhumaine Q)
100 *signet* the word was used to describe James I's own seal (*O.E.D.*)
100–102 lineation adjusted from Q
106 *o'er it* ed. (or't Q)
107 scarlet cloth would show through pale, fine cambric type linen covering it

Which these aspiring boys would climb upon;
He shall be released suddenly.

Enter Nobles

1 NOBLE
Good morning to your Grace.

DUKE
Welcome my lords.
[*The nobles kneel*]

2 NOBLE
Our knees shall take away the office of our feet for ever, 115
Unless your Grace bestow a father's eye
Upon the clouded fortunes of your son,
And in compassionate virtue grant him that
Which makes e'en mean men happy: liberty.

DUKE
[*Aside*] How seriously their loves and honours woo 120
For that which I am about to pray them do.—
Rise my lords, your knees sign his release:
We freely pardon him.

1 NOBLE
We owe your Grace much thanks, and he much duty.
Exeunt [*nobles*]

DUKE
It well becomes that judge to nod at crimes 125
That does commit greater himself and lives.
I may forgive a disobedient error
That expect pardon for adultery,
And in my old days am a youth in lust.
Many a beauty have I turned to poison 130
In the denial, covetous of all;
Age hot, is like a monster to be seen:
My hairs are white and yet my sins are green. [*Exit*]

Act III [Scene i]

Enter AMBITIOSO *and* SUPERVACUO

SUPERVACUO
Brother let my opinion sway you once;
I speak it for the best to have him die
Surest and soonest; if the signet come

122 *Rise my lords* ed. (Which, rise my lords Q)

126 cf. *King Lear* IV, vi: "handy dandy, which is the Justice, which is the thief?"

Unto the judge's hands, why then his doom
Will be deferred till sittings and Court-days, 5
Juries and further; faiths are bought and sold,
Oaths in these days are but the skin of gold.

AMBITIOSO
In troth 'tis true too.

SUPERVACUO
Then let's set by the judges
And fall to the officers; 'tis but mistaking
The duke our father's meaning, and where he named 10
"Ere many days" 'tis but forgetting that
And have him die i' the morning.

AMBITIOSO
Excellent!
Then am I heir—duke in a minute!

SUPERVACUO
Nay,
And he were once puffed out, here is a pin
Should quickly prick your bladder.

AMBITIOSO
Blest occasion! 15
He being packed we'll have some trick and wile
To wind our younger brother out of prison
That lies in for the rape; the lady's dead
And people's thoughts will soon be burièd.

SUPERVACUO
We may with safety do't and live and feed: 20
The duchess' sons are too proud to bleed.

AMBITIOSO
We are i' faith to say true. Come let's not linger—
I'll to the officers, go you before
And set an edge upon the executioner.

SUPERVACUO
Let me alone to grind him. *Exit*

AMBITIOSO
Meet; farewell. 25
I am next now, I rise just in that place
Where thou'rt cut off—upon thy neck kind brother;
The falling of one head lifts up another. *Exit*

11 no inverted commas in Q
15 *Blest* ed. (Blast Q)
24 *the executioner* the axe itself (Nicoll)
27 *cut off* ed. (cut of Q)

[Act III, Scene ii]

Enter with the nobles LUSSURIOSO *from prison*

LUSSURIOSO
My lords I am so much indebted to your loves
For this, oh this delivery.

1 NOBLE But our duties
My lord unto the hopes that grow in you.

LUSSURIOSO
If e'er I live to be myself I'll thank you.
Oh liberty thou sweet and heavenly dame! 5
But hell, for prison, is too mild a name! *Exeunt*

[Act III, Scene iii]

Enter AMBITIOSO *and* SUPERVACUO *with officers*

AMBITIOSO
Officers, here's the duke's signet, your firm warrant,
Brings the command of present death along with it
Unto our brother the duke's son; we are sorry
That we are so unnaturally employed
In such an unkind office, fitter far 5
For enemies than brothers.

SUPERVACUO But you know
The duke's command must be obeyed.

1 OFFICER
It must and shall my lord—this morning then,
So suddenly?

AMBITIOSO Ay alas poor good soul,
He must breakfast betimes, the executioner 10
Stands ready to put forth his cowardly valour.

2 OFFICER
Already?

SUPERVACUO
Already i' faith; oh sir destruction hies,
And that is least impudent, soonest dies.

1 OFFICER
Troth you say true my lord; we take our leaves. 15
Our office shall be found, we'll not delay

9 *poor good soul* hyphenated in Q
13 *Already* ed. (Alreardy Q)

The third part of a minute.

AMBITIOSO Therein you show
Yourselves good men and upright officers;
Pray let him die as private as he may,
Do him that favour, for the gaping people 20
Will but trouble him at his prayers
And make him curse and swear and so die black.
Will you be so far kind?

1 OFFICER It shall be done my lord.

AMBITIOSO
Why we do thank you; if we live to be,
You shall have a better office.

2 OFFICER Your good lordship. 25

SUPERVACUO
Commend us to the scaffold in our tears.

1 OFFICER
We'll weep and do your commendations. *Exeunt* [*officers*]

AMBITIOSO
Fine fools in office!

SUPERVACUO Things fall out so fit!

AMBITIOSO
So happily! Come brother ere next clock
His head will be made serve a bigger block. *Exeunt* 30

[Act III, Scene iv]

Enter [YOUNGER SON *and his prison* KEEPER]

YOUNGER SON
Keeper.

KEEPER My lord.

YOUNGER SON No news lately from our brothers?
Are they unmindful of us?

KEEPER
My lord a messenger came newly in
And brought this from 'em. [*He gives him a letter*]

YOUNGER SON Nothing but paper comforts?
I looked for my delivery before this; 5
Had they been worth their oaths—prithee be from us;
[*Exit* KEEPER]

3–4 lineation adjusted from Q

30 *block.* A pun on the sense of (i) execution block (ii) hat size.

Now, what say you forsooth? Speak out I pray:
[*He reads out the*] *letter*
"Brother be of good cheer"—
'Slud it begins like a whore with good cheer!
"Thou shalt not be long a prisoner"— 10
Not five and thirty year like a bankrupt, I think so!
"We have thought upon a device to get thee out by a trick"—
By a trick! Pox o' your trick and it be so long a playing.
"And so rest comforted, be merry and expect it suddenly"—
Be merry, hang merry, draw and quarter merry, I'll be mad! 15
Is't not strange that a man
Should lie in a whole month for a woman?
Well, we shall see how sudden our brothers
Will be in their promise, I must expect still a trick:
I shall not be long a prisoner. How now, what news? 20

[*Enter* KEEPER]

KEEPER
Bad news my lord, I am discharged of you.

YOUNGER SON
Slave, call'st thou that bad news! I thank you brothers.

KEEPER
My lord 'twill prove so; here come the officers
Into whose hands I must commit you. [*Exit* KEEPER]

YOUNGER SON
Ha, officers? What, why? 25

[*Enter* OFFICERS]

1 OFFICER
You must pardon us my lord,
Our office must be sound, here is our warrant,
The signet from the duke; you must straight suffer.

YOUNGER SON
Suffer? I'll suffer you to be gone, I'll suffer you
To come no more—what would you have me suffer? 30

15 possibly a s.d. here: *tears up letter*
16–20 prose in Q

7 s.d. in Q not printed as such; line 8 is italicised like subsequent quotations from the letter, but is preceded by the word "Letter" in roman thus:

Letter. *Brother be of . . .*

I follow Harrier in regarding "Letter" as a note to reader and actor, not to be spoken.

2 OFFICER
My lord those words were better changed to prayers,
The time's but brief with you; prepare to die.

YOUNGER SON
Sure 'tis not so.

3 OFFICER It is too true my lord.

YOUNGER SON
I tell you 'tis not, for the duke my father
Deferred me till next sitting, and I look 35
E'en every minute, threescore times an hour
For a release, a trick, wrought by my brothers.

1 OFFICER
A trick my lord? If you expect such comfort
Your hope's as fruitless as a barren woman:
Your brothers were the unhappy messengers 40
That brought this powerful token for your death.

YOUNGER SON
My brothers! No, no!

2 OFFICER 'Tis most true my lord.

YOUNGER SON
My brothers to bring a warrant for my death:
How strange this shows!

3 OFFICER There's no delaying time.

YOUNGER SON
Desire 'em hither, call 'em up, my brothers— 45
They shall deny it to your faces!

1 OFFICER My lord,
They're far enough by this, at least at Court,
And this most strict command they left behind 'em
When grief swum in their eyes: they showed like brothers,
Brim-full of heavy sorrow; but the duke 50
Must have his pleasure.

YOUNGER SON His pleasure?

1 OFFICER
These were their last words which my memory bears:
"Commend us to the scaffold in our tears".

YOUNGER SON
Pox dry their tears: what should I do with tears?
I hate 'em worse than any citizen's son 55

32 *brief* ed. (breife Q)
39 *hope's* ed. (hopes Q)
42, 43, 45 Harrier inconsistently uses the speech prefix *Brother* for *Son* by oversight
53 no inverted commas but in italic in Q

Can hate salt water. Here came a letter now,
New bleeding from their pens, scarce stinted yet—
Would I'd been torn in pieces when I tore it—
Look you officious whoresons, words of comfort:
"Not long a prisoner". 60

1 OFFICER
It says true in that sir, for you must suffer presently.

YOUNGER SON
A villainous Duns upon the letter: knavish exposition!
Look you then here sir: "We'll get thee out by a trick"
says he.

2 OFFICER
That may hold too sir, for you know
A trick is commonly four cards, which was meant 65
By us four officers.

YOUNGER SON Worse and worse dealing.

1 OFFICER
The hour beckons us,
The headsman waits: lift up your eyes to heaven.

YOUNGER SON
I thank you faith, good pretty wholesome counsel!
I should look up to heaven as you said 70
Whilst he behind me cozens me of my head!
Ay, that's the trick.

3 OFFICER You delay too long my lord.

YOUNGER SON
Stay good authority's bastards: since I must
Through brothers' perjury die, oh let me venom
Their souls with curses.

1 OFFICER Come 'tis no time to curse. 75

YOUNGER SON
Must I bleed then without respect of sign? Well—
My fault was sweet sport which the world approves;
I die for that which every woman loves. *Exeunt*

60 as 53
63 as 53
64–66 prose in Q
69 *pretty wholesome* ed. (pritty-holsome Q)

---

62 *Duns*. Duns Scotus the medieval scholastic philosopher became proverbial for foolishness.

76 G. B. Harrison remarks that medical bleeding had to be done under favourable astrological conditions.

[Act III, Scene v]

Enter VINDICE [*disguised*] *with* HIPPOLITO *his brother*

VINDICE
Oh sweet, delectable, rare, happy, ravishing!

HIPPOLITO
Why what's the matter brother?

VINDICE
Oh 'tis able
To make a man spring up and knock his forehead
Against yon silver ceiling.

HIPPOLITO
Prithee tell me
Why may not I partake with you? You vowed once 5
To give me share to every tragic thought.

VINDICE
By th' Mass I think I did too:
Then I'll divide it to thee. The old duke,
Thinking my outward shape and inward heart
Are cut out of one piece—for he that prates his secrets, 10
His heart stands o' the outside—hires me by price
To greet him with a lady
In some fit place veiled from the eyes o' the Court,
Some darkened blushless angle that is guilty
Of his forefathers' lusts, and great folks' riots; 15
To which I easily, to maintain my shape,
Consented, and did wish his impudent Grace
To meet her here in this unsunned lodge
Wherein 'tis night at noon, and here the rather
Because unto the torturing of his soul 20
The bastard and the duchess have appointed
Their meeting too in this luxurious circle—
Which most afflicting sight will kill his eyes
Before we kill the rest of him.

HIPPOLITO
'Twill i' faith, most dreadfully digested. 25
I see not how you could have missed me brother.

2–4 prose in Q
14 *guilty* in the sense of having witnessed guilty acts
16 *which I easily, to* ed. (which (I easily to . . . Q)

---

4 *silver ceiling*. Not only the sky above the open *Globe* theatre but also the painted "heavens", the canopy over the stage itself.
25 *digested*. i.e. worked out, planned; from the 1607 usage in Chemistry meaning "to bring to maturity by the action of heat" (*O.E.D.*).

VINDICE
True, but the violence of my joy forgot it.

HIPPOLITO
Ay; but where's that lady now?

VINDICE
Oh at that word
I'm lost again, you cannot find me yet,
I'm in a throng of happy apprehensions! 30
He's suited for a lady: I have took care
For a delicious lip, a sparkling eye:
You shall be witness brother,
Be ready, stand with your hat off. *Exit*

HIPPOLITO
Troth I wonder what lady it should be. 35
Yet 'tis no wonder now I think again
To have a lady stoop to a duke, that stoops unto his men:
'Tis common to be common, through the world,
And there's more private common shadowing vices
Than those who are known both by their names and prices. 40
'Tis part of my allegiance to stand bare
To the duke's concubine—and here she comes.

Enter VINDICE *with the skull of his love dressed up in tires*

VINDICE
Madam his Grace will not be absent long.
Secret? Ne'er doubt us madam. 'Twill be worth
Three velvet gowns to your ladyship. Known? 45
Few ladies respect that; disgrace? A poor thin shell!
'Tis the best grace you have to do it well;
I'll save your hand that labour, I'll unmask you.
[VINDICE *reveals the skull*]

HIPPOLITO
Why brother, brother.

VINDICE
Art thou beguiled now? Tut a lady can 50
At such, all hid, beguile a wiser man.
Have I not fitted the old surfeiter
With a quaint piece of beauty? Age and bare bone
Are e'er allied in action. Here's an eye
Able to tempt a great man—to serve God; 55
A pretty hanging lip, that has forgot now to dissemble.
Methinks this mouth should make a swearer tremble,
A drunkard clasp his teeth, and not undo 'em

46 *that; disgrace?* ed. (that? disgrace, Q)
54 pointing to the skull

To suffer wet damnation to run through 'em.
Here's a cheek keeps her colour, let the wind go whistle: 60
Spout rain, we fear thee not, be hot or cold
All's one with us. And is not he absurd
Whose fortunes are upon their faces set,
That fear no other God but wind and wet?

HIPPOLITO

Brother y'ave spoke that right. 65
Is this the form that, living, shone so bright?

VINDICE

The very same.
And now methinks I could e'en chide myself
For doting on her beauty, though her death
Shall be revenged after no common action. 70
Does the silkworm expend her yellow labours
For thee? For thee does she undo herself?
Are lordships sold to maintain ladyships
For the poor benefit of a bewitching minute?
Why does yon fellow falsify highways 75
And put his life between the judge's lips
To refine such a thing, keeps horse and men
To beat their valours for her?
Surely we're all mad people and they,
Whom we think are, are not: we mistake those. 80
'Tis we are mad in sense, they but in clothes.

HIPPOLITO

Faith and in clothes too we, give us our due.

VINDICE

Does every proud and self-affecting dame
Camphor her face for this, and grieve her maker
In sinful baths of milk, when many an infant starves 85
For her superfluous outside—all for this?
Who now bids twenty pound a night, prepares

62 *absurd* ed. (absur'd Q)
71 *yellow* i.e. bright, costly and rich as gold
72 *undo herself* i.e. exhaust herself *and* unwind the skein out of herself
84 *Camphor* the white aromatic base for cosmetics; hence, the cream itself

---

75 *falsify highways*. The economy of expression produces obscurity; broadly it means to make unsound, perhaps by altering signposts and diverting rich travellers into his predatory hands; but *falsify* may connote "make unsafe" and *fellow* may stand for "goodfellow", a thief or highwayman.

Music, perfumes and sweetmeats? All are hushed,
Thou may'st lie chaste now! It were fine methinks
To have thee seen at revels, forgetful feasts 90
And unclean brothels; sure 'twould fright the sinner
And make him a good coward, put a reveller
Out of his antic amble
And cloy an epicure with empty dishes.
Here might a scornful and ambitious woman 95
Look through and through herself; see, ladies, with false forms
You deceive men but cannot deceive worms.
Now to my tragic business. Look you brother,
I have not fashioned this only for show
And useless property, no—it shall bear a part 100
E'en in its own revenge. This very skull,
Whose mistress the duke poisoned with this drug,
The mortal curse of the earth, shall be revenged
In the like strain and kiss his lips to death.
As much as the dumb thing can, he shall feel; 105
What fails in poison we'll supply in steel.

HIPPOLITO

Brother I do applaud thy constant vengeance,
The quaintness of thy malice, above thought.

VINDICE

So 'tis laid on: now come and welcome duke,
I have her for thee. I protest it brother, 110
Methinks she makes almost as fair a sign
As some old gentlewoman in a periwig.
Hide thy face now for shame, thou hadst need have a mask now.
'Tis vain when beauty flows, but when it fleets
This would become graves better than the streets. 115

HIPPOLITO

You have my voice in that. Hark, the duke's come.
[*Noises within*]

VINDICE

Peace—let's observe what company he brings
And how he does absent 'em, for you know
He'll wish all private. Brother fall you back a little
With the bony lady.

93 *Out of* ed. (Out off Q) 101 *in its* ed. (in it Q)

90–97 Further episodes from the Dance of Death.

HIPPOLITO
That I will. [*He retires*]

VINDICE
So, so— 120
Now nine years vengeance crowd into a minute.

[*Enter the* DUKE *and gentlemen*]

DUKE
You shall have leave to leave us, with this charge:
Upon our lives, if we be missed by the duchess
Or any of the nobles, to give out
We're privately rid forth.

VINDICE
Oh happiness! 125

DUKE
With some few honourable gentlemen, you may say:
You may name those that are away from Court.

GENTLEMAN
Your will and pleasure shall be done my lord.
[*Exeunt gentlemen*]

VINDICE
Privately rid forth?
He strives to make sure work on't. [*Advances*] Your good
Grace. 130

DUKE
Piato! well done. Hast brought her? What lady is't?

VINDICE
Faith my lord a country lady, a little
Bashful at first as most of them are, but after
The first kiss my lord the worst is past with them:
Your Grace knows now what you have to do. She's some-
what 135
A grave look with her, but—

DUKE
I love that best, conduct her.

VINDICE
[*Aside*] Have at all.

DUKE
In gravest looks the greatest faults seem less:
Give me that sin that's robed in holiness.

VINDICE
[*Aside*] Back with the torch; brother raise the perfumes. 140

123 *the duchess* ed. (th Duchess Q)
132–136 prose in Q
135 *She's* ed. (sha's Q) = "she has"

---

136 *grave look* cf. *Romeo and Juliet* III, i where Mercutio, dying, jests "ask for me tomorrow, you shall find me a grave man".

DUKE
How sweet can a duke breathe? Age has no fault.
Pleasure should meet in a perfumed mist.
Lady, sweetly encountered: I came from Court,
I must be bold with you—oh! What's this? Oh!
[*He kisses the skull*]

VINDICE
Royal villain, white devil!

DUKE
Oh! 145

VINDICE
Brother—place the torch here that his affrighted eyeballs
May start into those hollows. Duke, dost know
Yon dreadful vizard? View it well; 'tis the skull
Of Gloriana, whom thou poisonedst last.

DUKE
Oh 't'as poisoned me! 150

VINDICE
Didst not know that till now?

DUKE
What are you two?

VINDICE
Villains all three! The very ragged bone
Has been sufficiently revenged.

DUKE
Oh Hippolito—call treason! [*Falls*]

HIPPOLITO
Yes my good lord. Treason, treason, treason! 155
Stamping on him

DUKE
Then I'm betrayed.

VINDICE
Alas poor lecher: in the hands of knaves
A slavish duke is baser than his slaves.

143–144 lineation adjusted from Q
145 *white devil* disguised devil
148 *vizard* deliberately ambiguous: face *and* mask

---

155 *Stamping on him.* As if he were the serpent or a damned soul being thrust into hell, a common subject for paintings and emblems (the Prologue tramples Envy in Jonson's *Poetaster*). Contrast the triumph over death and oblivion, who are trodden down and stamped on, in the titlepage to Raleigh's *History of the World*, 1614 (*Shakespeare's Poetics*, Plate VII) and cf. *Timon of Athens*

"I should fear those that dance before me now
Would one day stamp upon me" (I, ii).

DUKE
My teeth are eaten out.
VINDICE
Hadst any left?
HIPPOLITO
I think but few.
VINDICE
Then those that did eat are eaten.
DUKE
Oh my tongue! 160
VINDICE
Your tongue? 'Twill teach you to kiss closer,
Not like a slobbering Dutchman. You have eyes still:
Look, monster, what a lady hast thou made me
My once betrothed wife.
DUKE
Is it thou villain? Nay then—
VINDICE
'Tis I, 'tis Vindice, 'tis I! 165
HIPPOLITO
And let this comfort thee. Our lord and father
Fell sick upon the infection of thy frowns
And died in sadness. Be that thy hope of life.
DUKE
Oh!
VINDICE
He had his tongue, yet grief made him die speechless.
Puh, 'tis but early yet; now I'll begin 170
To stick thy soul with ulcers; I will make
Thy spirit grievous sore, it shall not rest
But like some pestilent man, toss in thy breast.
Mark me, duke,
Thou'rt a renowned, high, and mighty cuckold!
DUKE
Oh! 175
VINDICE
Thy bastard, thy bastard rides a-hunting in thy brow.
DUKE
Millions of deaths!
VINDICE
Nay to afflict thee more,
Here in this lodge they meet for damned clips:
Those eyes shall see the incest of their lips.
DUKE
Is there a hell besides this, villains?

162 *slobbering* ed. (Flobbering Q) a misreading of MS surely; Nicoll does not emend
174 realigned from Q and brackets removed

---

160 cf. *Hamlet* IV, iii "Not where he eats, but where he is eaten".

VINDICE
Villain? 180
Nay heaven is just, scorns are the hires of scorns,
I ne'er knew yet adulterer without horns.

HIPPOLITO
Once ere they die 'tis quitted. [*Noises within*]

VINDICE
Hark the music,
Their banquet is prepared, they're coming—

DUKE
Oh kill me not with that sight. 185

VINDICE
Thou shalt not lose that sight for all thy dukedom.

DUKE
Traitors, murderers!

VINDICE
What, is not thy tongue eaten out yet?
Then we'll invent a silence. Brother, stifle the torch.

DUKE
Treason! Murder! 190

VINDICE
Nay faith, we'll have you hushed now with thy dagger.
Nail down his tongue, and mine shall keep possession
About his heart; if he but gasp he dies,
We dread not death to quittance injuries. Brother,
If he but wink, not brooking the foul object 195
Let our two other hands tear up his lids
And make his eyes, like comets, shine through blood.
When the bad bleeds, then is the tragedy good.

HIPPOLITO
Whist brother, music's at our ear: they come.

Enter [SPURIO] *the bastard meeting the* DUCHESS

SPURIO
Had not that kiss a taste of sin 'twere sweet. 200

DUCHESS
Why there's no pleasure sweet but it is sinful.

186 *dukedom* ed. (duke-doome Q) 195 *object* objection

---

197 *The Atheist's Tragedy* contains several references to the significance of portents in the heavens as signs of divine anger, especially IV. iii, 164–167

"How can earth endure
The burden of this wickedness without
An earthquake, or the angry face of Heav'n
Be not enflam'd with lightning?"

SPURIO
True, such a bitter sweetness fate hath given;
Best side to us, is the worst side to heaven.

DUCHESS
Push, come, 'tis the old duke thy doubtful father—
The thought of him rubs heaven in thy way; 205
But I protest by yonder waxen fire,
Forget him or I'll poison him.

SPURIO
Madam you urge a thought which ne'er had life,
So deadly do I loathe him for my birth
That, if he took me hasped within his bed, 210
I would add murder to adultery
And with my sword give up his years to death.

DUCHESS
Why, now thou'rt sociable: let's in and feast.
Loudest music sound: pleasure is banquet's guest.
Exeunt [SPURIO *and* DUCHESS]

DUKE
I cannot brook— [*Dies*]

VINDICE
The brook is turned to blood. 215

HIPPOLITO
Thanks to loud music.

VINDICE
'Twas our friend indeed;
'Tis state, in music for a duke to bleed.
The dukedom wants a head, though yet unknown;
As fast as they peep up let's cut 'em down. *Exeunt*

[Act III, Scene vi]

Enter the duchess' two sons AMBITIOSO *and* SUPERVACUO

AMBITIOSO
Was not his execution rarely plotted?
We are the duke's sons now.

SUPERVACUO
Ay, you may thank my policy for that.

AMBITIOSO
Your policy for what?

206 *waxen fire* candle
214 *Loudest* ed. (Lowdst Q)
215 s.d. *Dies* ed. Perhaps this could be expanded to VINDICE *stabs him as he cries out and he dies*

SUPERVACUO
Why was't not my invention brother 5
To slip the judges, and, in lesser compass,
Did not I draw the model of his death,
Advising you to sudden officers
And e'en extemporal execution?

AMBITIOSO
Heart 'twas a thing I thought on too. 10

SUPERVACUO
You thought on't too! 'Sfoot slander not your thoughts
With glorious untruth: I know 'twas from you.

AMBITIOSO
Sir I say 'twas in my head.

[SUPERVACUO] Ay, like your brains then:
Ne'er to come out as long as you lived.

AMBITIOSO
You'd have the honour on't forsooth that your wit 15
Led him to the scaffold.

SUPERVACUO Since it is my due
I'll publish't—but I'll ha't, in spite of you.

AMBITIOSO
Methinks y'are much too bold, you should a little
Remember us brother, next to be honest duke.

SUPERVACUO
[*Aside*] Ay, it shall be as easy for you to be duke 20
As to be honest, and that's never i' faith.

AMBITIOSO
Well, cold he is by this time, and because
We're both ambitious be it our amity,
And let the glory be shared equally.

SUPERVACUO
I am content to that. 25

AMBITIOSO
This night our younger brother shall out of prison:
I have a trick.

SUPERVACUO A trick? Prithee what is't?

AMBITIOSO
We'll get him out by a wile.

SUPERVACUO Prithee what wile?

7 *model* ground plan 12 *from you* not in your mind
13 speech prefix SUPERVACUO ed. (*Spu.* Q)
16 *Led* ed. (lead Q)
17 punctuation adjusted to show that *but* = "indeed"
26 *our* ed. (out Q)

AMBITIOSO
No sir you shall not know it till it be done,
For then you'd swear 'twere yours.

[*Enter an officer with a bleeding head in his hand*]

SUPERVACUO
How now, what's he? 30

AMBITIOSO
One of the officers.

SUPERVACUO
Desired news.

AMBITIOSO
How now my friend?

OFFICER
My lords, under your pardon, I am allotted
To that desertless office to present you
With the yet bleeding head—

SUPERVACUO [*Aside*]
Ha! Ha! Excellent!

AMBITIOSO
[*Aside*] All's sure our own—brother canst weep thinkst thou? 35
'Twould grace our flattery much; think of some dame,
'Twill teach thee to dissemble.

SUPERVACUO
[*Aside*] I have thought—now for yourself.

AMBITIOSO
Our sorrows are so fluent
Our eyes o'erflow our tongues; words spoke in tears 40
Are like the murmurs of the waters, the sound
Is loudly heard but cannot be distinguished.

SUPERVACUO
How died he pray?

OFFICER
Oh full of rage and spleen.

SUPERVACUO
He died most valiantly then: we're glad to hear it.

OFFICER
We could not woo him once to pray. 45

AMBITIOSO
He showed himself a gentleman in that,
Give him his due.

OFFICER
But in the stead of prayer
He drew forth oaths.

SUPERVACUO
Then did he pray dear heart,
Although you understood him not.

OFFICER
My lords,
E'en at his last—with pardon be it spoke— 50
He cursed you both.

29 *till it* ed. (till't Q)   45 *woo* ed (woe Q)

SUPERVACUO He cursed us? 'Las, good soul.

AMBITIOSO
It was not in our powers, but the duke's pleasure.
[*Aside*] Finely dissembled o' both sides! Sweet fate,
Oh happy opportunity!

Enter LUSSURIOSO

LUSSURIOSO Now my lords—

AMBITIOSO & SUPERVACUO Oh!

LUSSURIOSO
Why do you shun me brothers? You may come nearer now, 55
The savour of the prison has forsook me,
I thank such kind lords as yourselves I'm free.

AMBITIOSO
Alive!

SUPERVACUO In health!

AMBITIOSO Released!
We were both e'en amazed with joy to see it.

LUSSURIOSO
I am much to thank you. 60

SUPERVACUO
Faith we spared no tongue unto my lord the duke.

AMBITIOSO
I know your delivery, brother,
Had not been half so sudden but for us.

SUPERVACUO
Oh how we pleaded.

LUSSURIOSO Most deserving brothers;
In my best studies I will think of it. *Exit* 65

AMBITIOSO
Oh death and vengeance!

SUPERVACUO Hell and torments!

AMBITIOSO Slave!
Cam'st thou to delude us?

OFFICER Delude you my lords?

SUPERVACUO
Ay villain: where's this head now?

OFFICER Why here my lord;
Just after his delivery you both came
With warrant from the duke to behead your brother. 70

55 realigned from Q

66–83 Highly reminiscent of the scenes in Marstonian comedy where characters attack and ridicule each other in *stychomythia*.

AMBITIOSO
Ay, our brother, the duke's son.

OFFICER
The duke's son my lord had his release before you came.

AMBITIOSO
Whose head's that, then?

OFFICER
His, whom you left command for—
Your own brother's.

AMBITIOSO
Our brother's? Oh furies!

SUPERVACUO
Plagues!

AMBITIOSO Confusions!

SUPERVACUO
Darkness!

AMBITIOSO
Devils! 75

SUPERVACUO
Fell it out so accursedly?

AMBITIOSO
So damnedly?

SUPERVACUO
Villain I'll brain thee with it!

OFFICER
Oh my good lord!

SUPERVACUO
The devil overtake thee!

AMBITIOSO
Oh fatal—

SUPERVACUO
Oh prodigious to our bloods!

AMBITIOSO
Did we dissemble?

SUPERVACUO
Did we make our tears women for thee? 80

AMBITIOSO
Laugh and rejoice for thee?

SUPERVACUO
Bring warrant for thy death?

AMBITIOSO
Mock off thy head?

SUPERVACUO
You had a trick,
You had a wile forsooth.

AMBITIOSO
A murrain meet 'em!
There's none of these wiles that ever come to good;
I see now there is nothing sure in mortality but mortality. 85
Well, no more words—shalt be revenged i' faith.
Come throw off clouds now brother; think of vengeance
And deeper settled hate. Sirrah sit fast:
We'll pull down all, but thou shalt down at last. *Exeunt*

83 *murrain* plague 83–87 prose in Q

Act IV, Scene i

Enter LUSSURIOSO *with* HIPPOLITO

LUSSURIOSO
Hippolito.
HIPPOLITO My lord: has your good lordship
Aught to command me in?
LUSSURIOSO I prithee leave us.
HIPPOLITO
How's this? Come, and leave us?
LUSSURIOSO Hippolito.
HIPPOLITO
Your honour, I stand ready for any dutious employment.
LUSSURIOSO
Heart, what mak'st thou here?
HIPPOLITO [*Aside*] A pretty lordly humour: 5
He bids me to be present; to depart;
Something has stung his honour.
LUSSURIOSO Be nearer, draw nearer;
You're not so good methinks, I'm angry with you.
HIPPOLITO
With me my lord? I'm angry with myself for't.
LUSSURIOSO
You did prefer a goodly fellow to me: 10
'Twas wittily elected, 'twas—I thought
He'd been a villain, and he proves a knave!
To me a knave!
HIPPOLITO I chose him for the best my lord:
'Tis much my sorrow if neglect in him
Breed discontent in you.
LUSSURIOSO Neglect? 'Twas will: judge of it: 15
Firmly to tell of an incredible act
Not to be thought, less to be spoken of,
'Twixt my stepmother and the bastard—oh,
Incestuous sweets between 'em!
HIPPOLITO Fie my lord.
LUSSURIOSO
I, in kind loyalty to my father's forehead, 20
Made this a desperate arm, and in that fury
Committed treason on the lawful bed

2 *Aught* ed. (ought Q)
6–7 realigned from Q
12 *He'd* ed. (Had Q) = "he had"

And with my sword e'en razed my father's bosom,
For which I was within a stroke of death.

HIPPOLITO
Alack, I'm sorry. [*Aside*] 'Sfoot, just upon the stroke 25
Jars in my brother: 'twill be villainous music!

Enter VINDICE [*disguised*]

VINDICE
My honoured lord.

LUSSURIOSO
Away prithee, forsake us: hereafter we'll not know thee.

VINDICE
Not know me my lord? Your lordship cannot choose.

LUSSURIOSO
Begone I say, thou art a false knave. 30

VINDICE
Why, the easier to be known my lord.

LUSSURIOSO
Push, I shall prove too bitter with a word,
Make thee a perpetual prisoner
And lay this ironage upon thee.

VINDICE [*Aside*] Mum,
For there's a doom would make a woman dumb. 35
Missing the bastard next him, the wind's come about;
Now 'tis my brother's turn to stay, mine to go out.

Exit VINDICE

LUSSURIOSO
Has greatly moved me.

HIPPOLITO Much to blame i' faith.

LUSSURIOSO
But I'll recover, to his ruin. 'Twas told me lately,
I know not whether falsely, that you'd a brother. 40

HIPPOLITO
Who I? Yes my good lord, I have a brother.

LUSSURIOSO
How chance the Court ne'er saw him? Of what nature?
How does he apply his hours?

23 *razed* ed. (rac'd Q)
23 *razed* grazed (as with a razor)
34 *ironage* ed. (yron-age Q) the spelling indicates two senses (i) fetters (ii) the imprisonment lasting an Age of Iron—*Harrier*
36 *come* ed. (comes Q)

---

52 A recurrence of the image from building: see I, iv, 68.

HIPPOLITO
Faith to curse Fates
Who, as he thinks, ordained him to be poor;
Keeps at home full of want and discontent. 45

LUSSURIOSO
There's hope in him, for discontent and want
Is the best clay to mould a villain of;
Hippolito, wish him repair to us;
If there be aught in him to please our blood
For thy sake we'll advance him, and build fair 50
His meanest fortunes; for it is in us
To rear up towers from cottages.

HIPPOLITO
It is so my lord; he will attend your honour,
But he's a man in whom much melancholy dwells.

LUSSURIOSO
Why the better: bring him to Court. 55

HIPPOLITO
With willingness and speed. [*Aside*] Whom he cast off
E'en now, must now succeed. Brother disguise must off;
In thine own shape now I'll prefer thee to him:
How strangely does himself work to undo him. *Exit*

LUSSURIOSO
This fellow will come fitly; he shall kill 60
That other slave that did abuse my spleen
And made it swell to treason. I have put
Much of my heart into him; he must die.
He that knows great men's secrets, and proves slight,
That man ne'er lives to see his beard turn white. 65
Ay, he shall speed him: I'll employ thee brother,
Slaves are but nails to drive out one another.
He being of black condition, suitable
To want and ill content, hope of preferment
Will grind him to an edge. 70

The nobles enter

1 NOBLE
Good days unto your honour.

47 *villain of* ed. (villaine off Q)
49 *aught* ed. (ought Q)
56–57 realigned from Q
68 *black* melancholic
70 Q prints the s.d. *The nobles enter* as the end of Lussurioso's speech, but all editors agree that it is a s.d. and emend accordingly

LUSSURIOSO
My kind lords,
I do return the like.

2 NOBLE
Saw you my lord the duke?

LUSSURIOSO
My lord and father: is he from Court?

1 NOBLE
He's su.e from Court, but where, which way his pleasure
Took, we know not nor can we hear on't. 75

[*Enter other nobles*]

LUSSURIOSO
Here come those should tell—saw you my lord and father?

3 NOBLE
Not since two hours before noon my lord,
And then he privately rid forth.

LUSSURIOSO
Oh he's rid forth.

1 NOBLE
'Twas wondrous privately.

2 NOBLE
There's none i' the Court had any knowledge on't. 80

LUSSURIOSO
His Grace is old, and sudden, 'tis no treason
To say the duke my father has a humour,
Or such a toy, about him; what in us
Would appear light, in him seems virtuous.

3 NOBLE
'Tis oracle my lord. *Exeunt* 85

[Act IV, Scene ii]

Enter VINDICE *and* HIPPOLITO (VINDICE *out of his disguise*)

HIPPOLITO
So, so, all's as it should be, y'are yourself.

VINDICE
How that great villain puts me to my shifts!

HIPPOLITO
He that did lately in disguise reject thee
Shall, now thou art thyself, as much respect thee.

VINDICE
'Twill be the quainter fallacy; but brother, 5
'Sfoot, what use will he put me to now, think'st thou?

74–76 realigned from Q 78 *rid* ed. (rod Q)
2 *great villain* ed. (great-villaine Q)

HIPPOLITO
Nay you must pardon me in that, I know not;
H'as some employment for you, but what 'tis
He and his secretary the devil knows best.

VINDICE
Well I must suit my tongue to his desires 10
What colour soe'er they be, hoping at last
To pile up all my wishes on his breast.

HIPPOLITO
Faith brother he himself shows the way.

VINDICE
Now the duke is dead the realm is clad in clay;
His death being not yet known, under his name 15
The people still are governed; well, thou his son
Art not long-lived, thou shalt not 'joy his death:
To kill thee then I should most honour thee,
For 'twould stand firm in every man's belief
Thou'st a kind child, and only diedst with grief. 20

HIPPOLITO
You fetch about well; but let's talk in present.
How will you appear in fashion different,
As well as in apparel, to make all things possible?
If you be but once tripped we fall for ever.
It is not the least policy to be doubtful; 25
You must change tongue—familiar was your first.

VINDICE
Why I'll bear me in some strain of melancholy
And string myself with heavy sounding wire
Like such an instrument that speaks merry things sadly.

HIPPOLITO
Then 'tis as I meant, I gave you out 30
At first in discontent.

VINDICE I'll turn myself, and then—

HIPPOLITO
'Sfoot here he comes—hast thought upon't?

VINDICE
Salute him, fear not me.

[*Enter* LUSSURIOSO]

LUSSURIOSO Hippolito.

HIPPOLITO
Your lordship.

21 *fetch about* produce witty paradoxes
22 *fashion* social background
32 *upon't?* ed. (uppont. Q)

LUSSURIOSO What's he yonder?

HIPPOLITO
'Tis Vindice my discontented brother, 35
Whom, 'cording to your will I've brought to Court.

LUSSURIOSO
Is that thy brother? Beshrew me a good presence;
I wonder h'as been from the Court so long.
Come nearer.

HIPPOLITO
Brother: lord Lussurioso the duke's son. 40

LUSSURIOSO
Be more near to us: welcome, nearer yet.

VINDICE
How don you? God you god den.

[VINDICE] *snatches off his hat and* [*bows*] *to him*

LUSSURIOSO We thank thee.
How strangely such a coarse, homely salute
Shows in the palace, where we greet in fire—
Nimble and desperate tongues! Should we name 45
God in a salutation 'twould ne'er be 'stood on't—heaven!
Tell me, what has made thee so melancholy.

VINDICE
Why going to law.

LUSSURIOSO
Why, will that make a man melancholy?

VINDICE
Yes, to look long upon ink and black buckram. I went me to 50
law in *anno quadragesimo secundo*, and I waded out of it in
anno sextagesimo tertio.

LUSSURIOSO
What, three and twenty years in law?

VINDICE
I have known those that have been five and fifty, and all
about pullin and pigs. 55

36 *'cording* ed. (cording Q)
I've ed. (I'ave Q)
40 *duke's* ed. (Duke Q)
42 s.d. [VINDICE] *snatches off his hat and* [*bows*] *to him* ed. (*Snatches of his hat and makes legs to him* Q)
43 *coarse, homely* ed. (course-homely Q)
51 *anno quadragesimo secundo* forty second year
52 *anno sextagesimo tertio* sixty third year
55 *pullin* poultry

LUSSURIOSO

May it be possible such men should breathe to vex the terms so much?

VINDICE

'Tis food to some my lord. There are old men at the present that are so poisoned with the affectation of law words, having had many suits canvassed, that their common talk is nothing 60 but Barbary Latin; they cannot so much as pray, but in law, that their sins may be removed with a writ of Error, and their souls fetched up to heaven with a sasarara.

[LUSSURIOSO]

It seems most strange to me;
Yet all the world meets round in the same bent: 65
Where the heart's set, there goes the tongue's consent.
How dost apply thy studies fellow?

VINDICE

Study? Why, to think how a great rich man lies a-dying, and a poor cobbler tolls the bell for him; how he cannot depart the world, and see the great chest stand before him; when he 70 lies speechless, how he will point you readily to all the boxes, and when he is past all memory, as the gossips guess, then thinks he of forfeitures and obligations. Nay, when to all men's hearings he whirls and rattles in the throat, he's busy threatening his poor tenants; and this would last me now 75 some seven years thinking, or thereabouts! But I have a conceit a-coming in picture upon this, I draw it myself, which i' faith la I'll present to your honour; you shall not choose but like it for your lordship shall give me nothing for it. 80

LUSSURIOSO

Nay you mistake me then,
For I am published bountiful enough;
Let's taste of your conceit.

56 *terms* sessions in which cases are heard
61 *Barbary* barbarous
63 *sasarara* writ of certiorari: appeal to the highest court against judgement below
64 LUSSURIOSO ed. (*Hip*. Q)
74 *whirls and rattles* ed. (whurles and rotles Q)

---

58 Uncorrected copies run this speech directly after Lussurioso's; corrected copies give it a fresh line. Lineation of the speech is altered accordingly but no other changes are made.

VINDICE
In picture my lord?
LUSSURIOSO
Ay, in picture.
VINDICE
Marry this it is:
"A usuring father to be boiling in hell, and his son and heir 85
with a whore dancing over him."
HIPPOLITO
[*Aside*] H'as pared him to the quick.
LUSSURIOSO
The conceit's pretty i' faith—
But take't upon my life 'twill ne'er be liked.
VINDICE
No? Why I'm sure the whore will be liked well enough! 90
HIPPOLITO
[*Aside*] Ay, if she were out o' the picture he'd like her then
himself.
VINDICE
And as for the son and heir, he shall be an eyesore to no
young revellers, for he shall be drawn in cloth of gold
breeches. 95
LUSSURIOSO
And thou hast put my meaning in the pockets
And canst not draw that out. My thought was this:
To see the picture of a usuring father
Boiling in hell—our rich men would ne'er like it.
VINDICE
Oh true, I cry you heartily mercy; I know the reason: for some 100
of 'em had rather be damned indeed than damned in colours.
LUSSURIOSO
[*Aside*] A parlous melancholy! H'as wit enough
To murder any man, and I'll give him means.—
I think thou art ill-moneyed?
VINDICE
Money! Ho, ho.

84 *picture* a moral emblem, condensing in this case the theme of several satiric comedies of the period
85–86 The words in inverted commas are printed in italic in Q
101 *in colours* in paint

---

85 cf. the fate of the merchant Barabas in Marlowe's *The Jew of Malta* and see Plate III in the Introduction.
96 *pockets.* Q corrected copies; uncorrected copies show the last three letters to have dropped into the next line.

'T'as been my want so long 'tis now my scoff; 105
I've e'en forgot what colour silver's of!

LUSSURIOSO
[*Aside*] It hits as I could wish.

VINDICE
I get good clothes
Of those that dread my humour, and for table room
I feed on those that cannot be rid of me.

LUSSURIOSO
[*Giving* VINDICE *money*] Somewhat to set thee up withal. 110

VINDICE
Oh mine eyes!

LUSSURIOSO How now man?

VINDICE Almost struck blind!
This bright unusual shine to me seems proud:
I dare not look till the sun be in a cloud.

LUSSURIOSO
[*Aside*] I think I shall affect his melancholy;—
How are they now?

VINDICE The better for your asking. 115

LUSSURIOSO
You shall be better yet if you but fasten
Truly on my intent. Now y'are both present
I will unbrace such a close private villain
Unto your vengeful swords, the like ne'er heard of,
Who hath disgraced you much and injured us. 120

HIPPOLITO
Disgraced us my lord?

LUSSURIOSO Ay, Hippolito.
I kept it here till now that both your angers
Might meet him at once.

VINDICE I'm covetous
To know the villain.

LUSSURIOSO You know him—that slave pandar
Piato, whom we threatened last 125
With irons in perpetual prisonment.

VINDICE
[*Aside*] All this is I!

HIPPOLITO Is't he my lord?

LUSSURIOSO
I'll tell you—you first preferred him to me.

106 *of!* ed. (off, Q)
112 *proud* too rich (Nicoll)
114 *affect* like
115 *your asking* ed. (you rasking Q)

VINDICE
Did you brother?
HIPPOLITO I did indeed.
LUSSURIOSO
And the ungrateful villain 130
To quit that kindness, strongly wrought with me,
Being as you see a likely man for pleasure,
With jewels to corrupt your virgin sister.
HIPPOLITO
Oh villain!
VINDICE He shall surely die that did it.
LUSSURIOSO
I, far from thinking any virgin harm, 135
Especially knowing her to be as chaste
As that part which scarce suffers to be touched,
The eye, would not endure him,—
VINDICE Would you not my lord?
'Twas wondrous honourably done.
LUSSURIOSO
But with some fine frowns kept him out.
VINDICE Out slave! 140
LUSSURIOSO
What did me he but in revenge of that
Went of his own free will to make infirm
Your sister's honour, whom I honour with my soul
For chaste respect; and, not prevailing there
—As 'twas but desperate folly to attempt it— 145
In mere spleen, by the way, waylays your mother,
Whose honour being a coward as it seems,
Yielded by little force.
VINDICE Coward indeed.
LUSSURIOSO
He, proud of their advantage, as he thought,
Brought me these news for happy; but I 150
—Heaven forgive me for't—
VINDICE What did your honour?
LUSSURIOSO
In rage pushed him from me,
Trampled beneath his throat, spurned him and bruised:
Indeed I was too cruel, to say truth.

131 *quit* repay
138 *The eye* ed. (Th'eye Q)
140 *fine* ed. (five Q)

HIPPOLITO
Most nobly managed. 155

VINDICE
[*Aside*] Has not heaven an ear? Is all the lightning wasted?

LUSSURIOSO
If I now were so impatient in a modest cause,
What should you be?

VINDICE
Full mad: he shall not live
To see the moon change.

LUSSURIOSO
He's about the palace.
Hippolito, entice him this way, that thy brother 160
May take full mark of him.

HIPPOLITO
Heart! That shall not need my lord,
I can direct him so far.

LUSSURIOSO
Yet for my hate's sake
Go, wind him this way; I'll see him bleed myself.

HIPPOLITO
[*Aside*] What now brother? 165

VINDICE
[*Aside*] Nay e'en what you will; y'are put to't, brother?

HIPPOLITO
[*Aside*] An impossible task I'll swear,
To bring him hither that's already here. *Exit* HIPPOLITO

LUSSURIOSO
Thy name? I have forgot it.

VINDICE
Vindice my lord.

LUSSURIOSO
'Tis a good name, that.

VINDICE
Ay, a revenger. 170

LUSSURIOSO
It does betoken courage, thou shouldst be valiant

162 *Heart!* ed. (Heart? Q) Nicoll conjectures that this is a compositor's error for *Marke?* but does not emend
171 *thou* ed. (thon Q)

---

156 *Is all the lightning wasted?* In *The Atheist's Tragedy* II. iv, 140–155 D'Amville and Borachio discuss the intervention of thunder in similar terms to Vindice's, though D'Amville is (foolishly) sceptical. Chettle's Hoffman has thunder's support:
"Ill acts move some, but myne's a cause that's right *Thunder and Lightning*
See the powers of heaven in apparitions/ . . . incensed" (I, i).
164 *wind him.* i.e. entice him subtly. Harrier conjectures "drive him down-wind by letting him scent you".

And kill thine enemies.

VINDICE
That's my hope my lord.

LUSSURIOSO
This slave is one.

VINDICE
I'll doom him.

LUSSURIOSO
Then I'll praise thee.
Do thou observe me best and I'll best raise thee.

Enter HIPPOLITO

VINDICE
Indeed I thank you. 175

LUSSURIOSO
Now Hippolito, where's the slave pandar?

HIPPOLITO
Your good lordship
Would have a loathsome sight of him, much offensive?
He's not in case now to be seen my lord,
The worst of all the deadly sins is in him: 180
That beggarly damnation, drunkenness.

LUSSURIOSO
Then he's a double slave.

VINDICE
[*Aside*] 'Twas well conveyed, upon a sudden wit.

LUSSURIOSO
What, are you both firmly resolved? I'll see him
Dead myself!

VINDICE
Or else let not us live. 185

LUSSURIOSO
You may direct your brother to take note of him.

HIPPOLITO
I shall.

LUSSURIOSO
Rise but in this and you shall never fall.

VINDICE
Your honour's vassals.

LUSSURIOSO [*Aside*]
This was wisely carried;
Deep policy in us makes fools of such: 190
Then must a slave die, when he knows too much.

Exit LUSSURIOSO

VINDICE
Oh thou almighty patience 'tis my wonder,

174 *observe* obey, follow
179 *in case* in a state; perhaps punning on *case* (= mask)
184–185 realigned from Q

That such a fellow, impudent and wicked,
Should not be cloven as he stood
Or with a secret wind burst open! 195
Is there no thunder left, or is't kept up
In stock for heavier vengeance? [*Thunder*] There it goes!

HIPPOLITO
Brother we lose ourselves.

VINDICE
But I have found it,
'Twill hold, 'tis sure, thanks, thanks to any spirit
That mingled it 'mongst my inventions.

HIPPOLITO
What is't? 200

VINDICE
'Tis sound and good, thou shalt partake it,
I'm hired to kill myself.

HIPPOLITO
True.

VINDICE
Prithee mark it;
And the old duke being dead but not conveyed
—For he's already missed too—and you know 205
Murder will peep out of the closest husk—

HIPPOLITO
Most true!

VINDICE
What say you then to this device:
If we dressed up the body of the duke—

HIPPOLITO
In that disguise of yours!

VINDICE
Y'are quick, y'ave reached it.

HIPPOLITO
I like it wondrously. 210

VINDICE
And being in drink, as you have published him,
To lean him on his elbow as if sleep had caught him
—Which claims most interest in such sluggy men.

HIPPOLITO
Good yet; but here's a doubt.
We, thought by th' duke's son to kill that pandar, 215
Shall, when he is known, be thought to kill the duke.

VINDICE
Neither, oh thanks! It is substantial;
For that disguise being on him, which I wore,

215 *We* ed. (Me Q)

---

197 *There it goes*. This recalls *The Atheist's Tragedy* II, iv.

It will be thought I, which he calls the pandar,
Did kill the duke and fled away in his 220
Apparel, leaving him so disguised
To avoid swift pursuit.

HIPPOLITO Firmer and firmer.

VINDICE
Nay doubt not, 'tis in grain, I warrant
It hold colour.

HIPPOLITO Let's about it.

VINDICE
But by the way too, now I think on't, brother, 225
Let's conjure that base devil out of our mother. *Exeunt*

[Act IV, Scene iii]

Enter the DUCHESS *arm in arm with the bastard* [SPURIO]*: he seemeth lasciviously to her; after them enter* SUPERVACUO *running with a rapier: his brother* [AMBITIOSO] *stops him*

SPURIO
Madam unlock yourself; should it be seen
Your arm would be suspected.

DUCHESS
Who is't that dares suspect or this, or these?
May not we deal our favours where we please?

SPURIO
I'm confident you may. *Exeunt* [SPURIO *and* DUCHESS] 5

AMBITIOSO
'Sfoot brother hold!

SUPERVACUO Would let the bastard shame us?

AMBITIOSO
Hold, hold brother! There's fitter time than now.

SUPERVACUO
Now, when I see it!

AMBITIOSO 'Tis too much seen already.

SUPERVACUO
Seen and known:
The nobler she is, the baser is she grown. 10

220–224 *Did kill . . . about it*: prose in Q
223 *in grain* set firm and hard (like paint or a well-fitted wooden joint)
6 *Would* ed. (Woult Q)
10 *she is* ed. (she's Q)

---

3 *this, or these.* Kisses or caresses (Harrier).

AMBITIOSO

If she were bent lasciviously—the fault
Of mighty women that sleep soft—Oh death
Must she needs choose such an unequal sinner
To make all worse?

SUPERVACUO

A bastard! The duke's bastard! Shame heaped on shame! 15

AMBITIOSO

Oh our disgrace!
Most women have small waist the world throughout,
But their desires are thousand miles about.

SUPERVACUO

Come, stay not here: let's after and prevent:
Or else they'll sin faster than we'll repent. *Exeunt* 20

[Act IV, Scene iv]

Enter VINDICE *and* HIPPOLITO *bringing out their mother* [GRATIANA,] *one by one shoulder, and the other by the other, with daggers in their hands*

VINDICE

O thou for whom no name is bad enough!

GRATIANA

What mean my sons? What, will you murder me?

VINDICE

Wicked, unnatural parent!

HIPPOLITO

Fiend of women!

GRATIANA

Oh! Are sons turned monsters? Help!

VINDICE

In vain.

GRATIANA

Are you so barbarous, to set iron nipples 5
Upon the breast that gave you suck?

VINDICE

That breast
Is turned to quarled poison.

17 *waist* ed. (waste Q) 18 *their* ed. (there Q)
2 *mean* ed. (meanes Q) 3 *parent* ed. (parents Q)
7 *quarled* usually used of curdled milk, hence "bitter"

19–20 Copies of Q in the first state reverse the order of lines 19 and 20 including the speech prefix *Sup*. and the stage direction *Exeunt*. Copies in the second state print the lines in the correct order, with speech prefix, but the stage direction is on line 18. I have emended this remaining error.

GRATIANA
Cut not your days for't: am not I your mother?
VINDICE
Thou dost usurp that title now by fraud,
For in that shell of mother breeds a bawd. 10
GRATIANA
A bawd! Oh name far loathsomer than hell!
HIPPOLITO
It should be so, knew'st thou thy office well.
GRATIANA
I hate it.
VINDICE
Ah is't possible, you powers on high,
That women should dissemble when they die? 15
GRATIANA
Dissemble?
VINDICE Did not the duke's son direct
A fellow of the world's condition hither
That did corrupt all that was good in thee,
Made thee uncivilly forget thyself
And work our sister to his lust?
GRATIANA Who, I? 20
That had been monstrous? I defy that man
For any such intent. None lives so pure
But shall be soiled with slander—
Good son believe it not.
VINDICE Oh I'm in doubt
Whether I'm myself or no! 25

12 *knewst* Q; but uncorrected copies read *knowst*

---

8 *cut not your days*. i.e. "lessen not your life" referring to II. ii, 96 where *Exodus*, xx, 12 is invoked.
14 Q reads "Ah ist possible, *Thou onely*, you powers on hie,". Nicoll emends to
"Ah ist possible, you [heavenly] powers on hie"
and Price (in *The Library* 5th series XV 1962) suggests that originally the line read
"Ah ist possible Thou onely God on hie"
but either Eld or the previous owner crossed out "God" and wrote in, above, "you powers". The printer set "Thou onely" in italic instead of deleting the whole phrase. I have accordingly emended this error, though for stylistic reasons I would have preferred the conjectural original state of the line: "Ah ist possible Thou onely God on hie". "God" would have been scored out because of fears that it seem too profane.

Stay—let me look again upon this face:
Who shall be saved when mothers have no grace?

HIPPOLITO
'Twould make one half despair.

VINDICE
I was the man:
Defy me now! Let's see: do't modestly.

GRATIANA
Oh hell unto my soul. 30

VINDICE
In that disguise, I, sent from the duke's son,
Tried you, and found you base metal
As any villain might have done.

GRATIANA
Oh no: no tongue but yours could have bewitched me so.

VINDICE
Oh nimble in damnation, quick in tune: 35
There is no devil could strike fire so soon!
I am confuted in a word.

GRATIANA
Oh sons forgive me, to myself I'll prove more true;
You that should honour me—I kneel to you.
[*She kneels and weeps*]

VINDICE
A mother to give aim to her own daughter! 40

HIPPOLITO
True brother: how far beyond nature 'tis,
Though many mothers do't!

VINDICE
Nay and you draw tears once, go you to bed;
Wet will make iron blush and change to red:

41 *'tis* Q; but uncorrected copies read *to't* which is nonsense though rhyming with l. 42

---

44 This line exists in three states:
(i) Wee will make you blush and change to red
(ii) Wet will make you blush and change to red
(iii) Wet will make yron blush and change to red
I am indebted to Price, in his article already cited, for information about the second state. I print the last state because it makes the best sense in the context, though it is perfectly possible that compositor's corrections went from the third to the first. Harrier prints (i) and Sālgādo follows him without any explanation. Only Symonds prints (ii).

44 *red.* Caused by rust; cf. Othello's order
"Put up
Your bright swords for the dew will rust them".

Brother it rains, 'twill spoil your dagger, house it. 45

HIPPOLITO

'Tis done.

VINDICE

I' faith 'tis a sweet shower, it does much good;
The fruitful grounds and meadows of her soul
Has been long dry. Pour down, thou blessed dew.
Rise mother; troth this shower has made you higher. 50

GRATIANA

Oh you heavens, take this infectious spot out of my soul!
I'll rinse it in seven waters of mine eyes;
Make my tears salt enough to taste of grace;
To weep is to our sex naturally given,
But to weep truly—that's a gift from heaven! 55

VINDICE

Nay I'll kiss you now; kiss her, brother,
Let's marry her to our souls, wherein's no lust,
And honourably love her.

HIPPOLITO Let it be.

VINDICE

For honest women are so seld and rare,
'Tis good to cherish those poor few that are. 60
Oh you of easy wax, do but imagine
Now the disease has left you, how leprously
That office would have clinged unto your forehead.
All mothers that had any graceful hue
Would have worn masks to hide their face at you. 65
It would have grown to this, at your foul name
Green coloured maids would have turned red with shame.

HIPPOLITO

And then, our sister full of hire and baseness—

VINDICE

There had been boiling lead again!
The duke's son's great concubine! 70

59 *seld* ed. (sild Q)
59 *seld* seldom found
68 i.e. "our sister, a complete whore, ignoble and base"
70 *The duke's* Q; but uncorrected copies read *Duke's*

---

45 *it rains.* A reference to Gratiana's tears.
67 *Green coloured maids.* Very young girls; the greenness was "emblemized as a sign of lovesickness or vague desire" (Partridge, *Shakespeare's Bawdy*, p. 123), there is a possible reference also to anaemic complexions of adolescence.

A drab of state, a cloth o' silver slut,
To have her train borne up and her soul
Trail i' the dirt: great!

HIPPOLITO
To be miserably great:
Rich, to be eternally wretched.

VINDICE
O common madness: 75
Ask but the thriving'st harlot in cold blood,
She'd give the world to make her honour good.
Perhaps you'll say, but only to the duke's son
In private—why, she first begins with one
Who afterward to thousand proves a whore: 80
"Break ice in one place it will crack in more."

GRATIANA
Most certainly applied!

HIPPOLITO
Oh brother you forget our business.

VINDICE
And well remembered; joy's a subtle elf,
I think man's happiest when he forgets himself. 85
Farewell once dried, now holy-watered mead:
Our hearts wear feathers that before wore lead.

GRATIANA
I'll give you this: that one I never knew
Plead better for, and 'gainst the devil, than you.

VINDICE
You make me proud on't. 90

73 *To be* Q but uncorrected copies read *Too*
78 *to the* ed. (to'th Q)
86 addressed to Gratiana

72–74 Realigned from Q; Harrier prints as one line *To have . . . dirt* and omits *great* apparently following Collier who observes "the word *great* is added to the 4° in this line, but it belongs to Hippolito, and what he says has been hitherto misprinted". There are two states to Hippolito's line:

(i) To be miserably great
(ii) Too miserably great

Firstly there is no warrant for omitting *great* at the end of Vindice's speech, and, granting its presence, we see that the balance of an antithesis depends on it:

"great . . . miserably great: Rich . . . eternally wretched"

both the words *great* and *rich* are subjected to analysis, with the same conclusion in each case. Nicoll prints accurately and I follow him, only adjusting lineation.

HIPPOLITO
Commend us in all virtue to our sister.
VINDICE
Ay for the love of heaven, to that true maid.
GRATIANA
With my best words.
VINDICE Why that was motherly said.
Exeunt [VINDICE *and* HIPPOLITO]
GRATIANA
I wonder now what fury did transport me;
I feel good thoughts begin to settle in me. 95
Oh with what forehead can I look on her
Whose honour I've so impiously beset
—And here she comes.

[*Enter* CASTIZA]

CASTIZA
Now mother you have wrought with me so strongly
That what for my advancement, as to calm 100
The trouble of your tongue, I am content—
GRATIANA
Content to what?
CASTIZA To do as you have wished me,
To prostitute my breast to the duke's son
And put myself to common usury.
GRATIANA
I hope you will not so.
CASTIZA Hope you I will not? 105
That's not the hope you look to be saved in.
GRATIANA
Truth but it is.
CASTIZA Do not deceive yourself:
I am, as you, e'en out of marble wrought:
What would you now, are ye not pleased yet with me?
You shall not wish me to be more lascivious 110
Than I intend to be.
GRATIANA Strike not me cold.
CASTIZA
How often have you charged me on your blessing
To be a cursed woman! When you knew
Your blessing had no force to make me lewd
You laid your curse upon me. That did more 115

96 *forehead* dignity or pride

—The mother's curse is heavy; where that fights,
Sons set in storm and daughters lose their lights.

GRATIANA

Good child, dear maid, if there be any spark
Of heavenly intellectual fire within thee,
Oh let my breath revive it to a flame: 120
Put not all out with woman's wilful follies,
I am recovered of that foul disease
That haunts too many mothers: kind, forgive me,
Make me not sick in health. If then
My words prevailed when they were wickedness, 125
How much more now when they are just and good!

CASTIZA

I wonder what you mean: are not you she
For whose infect persuasions I could scarce
Kneel out my prayers, and had much ado
In three hours' reading to untwist so much 130
Of the black serpent as you wound about me?

GRATIANA

'Tis unfruitful child, tedious, to repeat what's past:
I'm now your present mother.

CASTIZA Push, now 'tis too late.

GRATIANA

Bethink again, thou know'st not what thou say'st.

CASTIZA

No—deny advancement, treasure, the duke's son? 135

GRATIANA

Oh see, I spoke those words, and now they poison me:
What will the deed do then?
Advancement? True: as high as shame can pitch;
For treasure? Who e'er knew a harlot rich
Or could build by the purchase of her sin 140
An hospital to keep their bastards in?
The duke's son! Oh when women are young courtiers
They are sure to be old beggars;

119–120 realigned from Q
123 *kind, forgive* ed. (kind forgive Q) the comma emphasises that *kind* = "kind daughter"
141–143 realigned from Q

---

132 *unfruitful child, tedious,* ed. (unfruitful, held tedious Q). Collins first made this emendation and was followed by Symonds and Harrier; but Nicoll and Sālgado reproduce the Q reading.

To know the miseries most harlots taste
Thou'd'st wish thyself unborn when thou art unchaste. 145

CASTIZA
Oh mother let me twine about your neck
And kiss you till my soul melt on your lips:
I did but this to try you.

GRATIANA
Oh speak truth!

CASTIZA
Indeed I did not; for no tongue has force
To alter me from honest. 150
If maidens would, men's words could have no power;
A virgin honour is a crystal tower
Which being weak is guarded with good spirits:
Until she basely yields no ill inherits.

GRATIANA
Oh happy child! Faith and thy birth hath saved me. 155
'Mongst thousand daughters happiest of all others!
Be thou a glass for maids, and I for mothers. *Exeunt*

[Act V, Scene i]

Enter VINDICE *and* HIPPOLITO [*with the duke's corpse*]

VINDICE
So, so, he leans well; take heed you wake him not brother.

HIPPOLITO
I warrant you, my life for yours.

VINDICE
That's a good lay, for I must kill myself! [*Points to corpse*]
Brother that's I: that sits for me: do you mark it. And I must
stand ready here to make away myself yonder; I must sit to 5
be killed, and stand to kill myself—I could vary it not so little

149 *I did not* i.e. did not speak truth
149–150 realigned from Q
157 *Be* ed. (Buy Q) the emendation of Reed in the 1780 edition of *Dodsley's Old English Plays*
6 *vary* ed. (varry Q)

1 s.d. The farcical stage business involving the duke's corpse recalls Act IV of *The Jew of Malta* where Barabas and Ithamore strangle Friar Barnadine, prop him up with his own staff "as if he were begging of bacon" and watch from concealment as Friar Jacomo supposes him to be barring the way and assaults him with a staff. Barabas then steps forth and accuses the friar of murder.

as thrice over again, 't'as some eight returns like Michaelmas Term.

HIPPOLITO

That's enow, o' conscience.

VINDICE

But sirrah does the duke's son come single? 10

HIPPOLITO

No, there's the hell on't, his faith's too feeble to go alone. He brings flesh-flies after him that will buzz against supper time, and hum for his coming out.

VINDICE

Ah the fly-flop of vengeance beat 'em to pieces! Here was the sweetest occasion, the fittest hour to have made my revenge 15 familiar with him—show him the body of the duke his father, and how quaintly he died like a politician in hugger-mugger —made no man acquainted with it, and in catastrophe slain him over his father's breast! And oh I'm mad to lose such a sweet opportunity. 20

HIPPOLITO

Nay push, prithee be content! There's no remedy present; may not hereafter times open in as fair faces as this?

VINDICE

They may if they can paint so well.

HIPPOLITO

Come now, to avoid all suspicion let's forsake this room and be going to meet the duke's son. 25

VINDICE

Content, I'm for any weather. Heart, step close, here he comes!

Enter LUSSURIOSO

HIPPOLITO

My honoured lord.

LUSSURIOSO

Oh me—you both present.

17 *he died* Q corrected copies *he did* uncorrected copies
18 *catastrophe* conclusion

---

7 *eight returns.* A return was an officer's report confirming the execution of a writ or Court Order; Michaelmas Term lasts eight weeks. The weak jest is meant for lawyers or young students of the Inns of Court, whose presence in the audience resulted in a mass of such detailed references to legal matters in Jacobean plays.

17 *like a politician in hugger-mugger.* i.e. "quickly and secretly like a Machiavel"; also recalling the usage in *Hamlet* IV, v.

VINDICE
E'en newly my lord, just as your lordship entered now. 30
About this place we had notice given he should be, but in some loathsome plight or other.

HIPPOLITO
Came your honour private?

LUSSURIOSO
Private enough for this: only a few attend my coming out.

HIPPOLITO
[*Aside*] Death rot those few! 35

LUSSURIOSO
Stay—yonder's the slave.

VINDICE
Mass there's the slave indeed my lord;
[*Aside*] 'Tis a good child, he calls his father slave!

LUSSURIOSO
Ay, that's the villain, the damned villain! Softly,
Tread easy.

VINDICE Puh, I warrant you my lord, 40
We'll stifle in our breaths.

LUSSURIOSO That will do well.
Base rogue thou sleepest thy last! [*Aside*] 'Tis policy
To have him killed in's sleep, for if he waked
He would betray all to them.

VINDICE But my lord—

LUSSURIOSO Ha? What say'st?

VINDICE
Shall we kill him now he's drunk?

LUSSURIOSO Ay, best of all. 45

VINDICE
Why then he will ne'er live to be sober.

LUSSURIOSO
No matter: let him reel to hell.

VINDICE
But being so full of liquor I fear he will put out all the fire!

LUSSURIOSO
Thou art a mad breast!

VINDICE
[*Aside*] And leave none to warm your lordship's gols withall. 50

40 *Puh* Q; but Harrier and Salgado read *Push*
49 *breast* Q corrected copies *beast* uncorrected copies
50 *gols* hands—common vernacular

—For he that dies drunk falls into hell fire like a bucket o' water: qush, qush.

LUSSURIOSO

Come, be ready, nake your swords, think of your wrongs: this slave has injured you.

VINDICE

Troth so he has, and he has paid well for't. 55

LUSSURIOSO

Meet with him now.

VINDICE You'll bear us out my lord?

LUSSURIOSO

Puh, am I a lord for nothing think you?
Quickly now!

VINDICE Sa, sa, sa, thump! [*He stabs the corpse*] There he lies!

LUSSURIOSO

Nimbly done. [*Approaches the corpse*] Ha! Oh villains, murderers,
'Tis the old duke my father!

VINDICE [*Aside*] That's a jest. 60

LUSSURIOSO

What, stiff and cold already?
Oh pardon me to call you from your names,
'Tis none of your deed; that villain Piato
Whom you thought now to kill has murdered him
And left him thus disguised.

HIPPOLITO And not unlikely. 65

VINDICE

Oh rascal, was he not ashamed
To put the duke into a greasy doublet?

LUSSURIOSO

He has been cold and stiff—who knows how long?

VINDICE

[*Aside*] Marry that do I!

LUSSURIOSO

No words I pray, off anything intended! 70

VINDICE

Oh my lord.

HIPPOLITO

I would fain have your lordship think that we
Have small reason to prate.

53 *nake* draw
53 *nake* Q corrected copies *make* uncorrected

LUSSURIOSO
Faith thou sayest true. I'll forthwith send to Court
For all the nobles, bastard, duchess, all— 75
How here by miracle we found him dead
And, in his raiment, that foul villain fled.

VINDICE
That will be the best way my lord, to clear
Us all; let's cast about to be clear.

LUSSURIOSO
Ho! Nencio, Sordido, and the rest! 80

Enter all [his attendants]

1 ATTENDANT
My lord.

2 ATTENDANT My lord.

LUSSURIOSO
Be witnesses of a strange spectacle.
Choosing for private conference that sad room
We found the duke my father 'gealed in blood.

1 ATTENDANT
My lord the duke! Run, hie thee Nencio, 85
Startle the Court by signifying so much. [*Exit* NENCIO]

VINDICE
[*Aside*] This much by wit a deep revenger can:
When murder's known, to be the clearest man.
We're farthest off, and with as bold an eye
Survey his body as the standers-by. 90

LUSSURIOSO
My royal father, too basely let blood
By a malevolent slave!

HIPPOLITO [*Aside*] Hark! He calls thee
Slave again.

VINDICE [*Aside*] H'as lost, he may!

LUSSURIOSO Oh sight,
Look hither, see, his lips are gnawn with poison!

VINDICE
How? His lips? By the Mass, they be! 95

81 1 ATTENDANT ed. (1. Q)
2 ATTENDANT ed. (2. Q)
84 *'gealed* stiff and covered in congealed blood
89 *farthest* ed. (fordest Q)
93 *H'as* ed. (Ha's Q)
94 *poison!* ed. (poisō. Q)
95 *By the Mass* ed. (By'th masse Q)

LUSSURIOSO
Oh villain—Oh rogue—Oh slave—Oh rascal!
HIPPOLITO
[*Aside*] Oh good deceit!—He quits him with like terms.
1 VOICE WITHIN
Where?
2 VOICE WITHIN Which way?

[*Enter* AMBITIOSO *and* SUPERVACUO *with nobles and gentlemen*]

AMBITIOSO
Over what roof hangs this prodigious comet
In deadly fire?
LUSSURIOSO Behold, behold my lords: 100
The duke my father's murdered by a vassal
That owes this habit, and here left disguised.

[*Enter the* DUCHESS *and* SPURIO]

DUCHESS
My lord and husband!
2 NOBLE Reverend majesty.
1 NOBLE
I have seen these clothes often attending on him.
VINDICE
[*Aside*] That nobleman has been in the country, for he does 105
not lie.
SUPERVACUO
[*Aside*] Learn of our mother—let's dissemble too!
I am glad he's vanished: so I hope are you?
AMBITIOSO
[*Aside*] Ay, you may take my word for't.
SPURIO Old dad dead?
Ay, one of his cast sins will send the fates 110
Most hearty commendations by his own son;

98 1 VOICE WITHIN ed. (1. Q)
2 VOICE WITHIN ed. (2. Q)
102 *owes* owns
107 *too* ed. (to Q)

---

99 *prodigious comet.* A commonplace in Elizabethan drama is the idea that commotions in the heavens presage doom; cf. *I Henry VI* I. i, 2–3
"Comets, importing change of times and states,
Brandish your crystal tresses in the sky".
Ribner discusses the subject in relation to *The Atheist's Tragedy* (pp. xliii–xlix), Henry Chettle's *Hoffman* has several such references.

I'll tug in the new stream till strength be done.

LUSSURIOSO

Where be those two that did affirm to us
My lord the duke was privately rid forth?

1 GENTLEMAN

Oh pardon us my lords, he gave that charge 115
Upon our lives, if he were missed at Court,
To answer so. He rode not anywhere,
We left him private with that fellow, here.

VINDICE

[*Aside*] Confirmed.

LUSSURIOSO

Oh heavens, that false charge was his death. 120
Impudent beggars! Durst you to our face
Maintain such a false answer? Bear him straight
To execution.

1 GENTLEMAN My lord!

LUSSURIOSO Urge me no more.

In this, the excuse may be called half the murder.

VINDICE

[*Aside*] You've sentenced well.

LUSSURIOSO Away, see it be done. 125

[*Exit* 1 GENTLEMAN *under guard*]

VINDICE

[*Aside*] Could you not stick? See what confession doth.
Who would not lie when men are hanged for truth?

HIPPOLITO

[*Aside*] Brother, how happy is our vengeance!

VINDICE [*Aside*] Why, it hits

Past the apprehension of indifferent wits.

LUSSURIOSO

My lord let post horse be sent 130
Into all places to entrap the villain.

VINDICE

[*Aside*] Post horse! Ha ha.

1 NOBLE

My lord we're something bold to know our duty.
Your father's accidentally departed,
The titles that were due to him meet you. 135

LUSSURIOSO

Meet me? I'm not at leisure my good lord,

115 1 GENTLEMAN ed. (1. Q)
126 *Could you not stick* i.e. "could you not remain firm in purpose"
133 1 NOBLE ed. (*Nob.* Q)

I've many griefs to dispatch out o' the way.—
[*Aside*] Welcome sweet titles!—Talk to me my lords
Of sepulchres and mighty emperors' bones,
That's thought for me. 140

VINDICE
[*Aside*] So, one may see by this how foreign markets go:
Courtiers have feet o' the nines and tongues o' the twelves:
They flatter dukes, and dukes flatter themselves.

2 NOBLE
My lord it is your shine must comfort us.

LUSSURIOSO
Alas I shine in tears like the sun in April. 145

1 NOBLE
You're now my lord's Grace.

LUSSURIOSO
My lord's Grace? I perceive you'll have it so.

2 NOBLE
'Tis but your own.

LUSSURIOSO Then heavens give me grace to be so.

VINDICE
[*Aside*] He prays well for himself!

1 NOBLE Madam all sorrows
Must run their circles into joys; no doubt but time 150
Will make the murderer bring forth himself.

VINDICE
[*Aside*] He were an ass then i' faith!

1 NOBLE In the mean season
Let us bethink the latest funeral honours
Due to the duke's cold body; and, withall,
Calling to memory our new happiness 155
Spread in his royal son,—lords, gentlemen,
Prepare for revels!

VINDICE [*Aside*] Revels!

142 *feet . . . nines . . . tongues . . . twelves* tongues three sizes larger than feet
144 2 NOBLE ed. (*Nob.* Q) 146 1 NOBLE ed. (*Nobl.* Q)
148 2 NOBLE ed. (*Nobl.* Q) 149 1 NOBLE ed. (*Nobl.* Q)
152 1 NOBLE ed. (*Nob.* Q)

---

141 *foreign markets.* Perhaps referring to the market for titles in Jacobean England: James I gave away and sold huge numbers of knighthoods and baronetcies.

1 NOBLE Time hath several falls:
Griefs lift up joys, feasts put down funerals.

LUSSURIOSO
Come then my lords, my favours to you all.
[*Aside*] The duchess is suspected foully bent; 160
I'll begin dukedom with her banishment.
Exeunt [LUSSURIOSO] *nobles and* DUCHESS

HIPPOLITO
[*Aside*] Revels.

VINDICE
[*Aside*] Ay that's the word. We are firm yet:
Strike one strain more and then we crown our wit.
Exeunt [VINDICE *and* HIPPOLITO]

SPURIO
Well, have the fairest mark— 165
So said the duke when he begot me—
And if I miss his heart or near about
Then have at any—a bastard scorns to be out. [*Exit*]

SUPERVACUO
Not'st thou that Spurio, brother?

AMBITIOSO
Yes I note him, to our shame.

SUPERVACUO He shall not 170
Live: his hair shall not grow much longer.
In this time of revels tricks may be set afoot.
Seest thou yon new moon? It shall outlive
The new duke by much: this hand shall dispossess
Him: then we're mighty. 175
A mask is treason's licence: that build upon—
'Tis murder's best face, when a vizard's on!
Exit SUPERVACUO

AMBITIOSO
Is't so? 'Tis very good:
And do you think to be duke then, kind brother?
I'll see fair play: drop one, and there lies t'other. 180
Exit AMBITIOSO

157 1 NOBLE ed. (*Nobl.* Q)
157 *Time . . . falls* changes or disguises (Nicoll)
161 s.d. *Exeunt* [LUSSURIOSO] *nobles* ed. (*Exeunt Duke Nobles* Q)
164 s.d. *Exeunt* [VINDICE *and* HIPPOLITO] ed. (*Exeu.* Bro. Q)
166 bracketed in Q 170–175 prose in Q 178 *'Tis* ed. ('ts Q)

---

169 Nicoll gives this speech to Ambitioso because he thinks it out of character for Supervacuo, and changes the other relevant speech headings in the scene from here on.

[Act V, Scene ii]

Enter VINDICE *and* HIPPOLITO *with* PIERO *and other lords*

VINDICE

My lords be all of music! Strike old griefs into other countries
That flow in too much milk and have faint livers,
Not daring to stab home their discontents.
Let our hid flames break out as fire, as lightning,
To blast this villainous dukedom vexed with sin: 5
Wind up your souls to their full height again.

PIERO

How?

1 LORD Which way?

3 LORD Any way! Our wrongs are such,
We cannot justly be revenged too much.

VINDICE

You shall have all enough. Revels are toward,
And those few nobles that have long suppressed you 10
Are busied to the furnishing of a mask
And do affect to make a pleasant tale on't.
The masking suits are fashioning; now comes in
That which must glad us all: we to take pattern
Of all those suits, the colour, trimming, fashion, 15
E'en to an undistinguished hair almost.
Then entering first, observing the true form,
Within a strain or two we shall find leisure
To steal our swords out handsomely,
And when they think their pleasure sweet and good, 20
In midst of all their joys they shall sigh blood!

PIERO

Weightily, effectually!

12 *affect* desire
16 *hair* wig, or possibly the proverbial "to a hair" = to the smallest detail

---

6 *Wind up*. The metaphor may be taken from a crossbow or windlass, as Harrier suggests; but there may be an echo of Lady Macbeth

"But screw your courage to the sticking place
And we'll not fail" (*Macbeth* I, vii)

where the reference is to tightening the strings of a musical instrument and hence to tightening the heart-strings.

3 LORD Before the other maskers come—
VINDICE
We're gone, all done and past.
PIERO
But how for the duke's guard?
VINDICE Let that alone:
By one and one their strengths shall be drunk down. 25
HIPPOLITO
There are five hundred gentlemen in the action
That will apply themselves and not stand idle.
PIERO
Oh let us hug your bosoms!
VINDICE Come my lords,
Prepare for deeds, let other times have words. *Exeunt*

[Act V, Scene iii]

In a dumb show: the possessing of the young duke [LUSSURIOSO] *with all his nobles; then sounding music, a furnished table is brought forth, then enters* [LUSSURIOSO] *and his nobles to the banquet. A blazing star appeareth.*

1 NOBLE
Many harmonious hours and choicest pleasures
Fill up the royal numbers of your years.
LUSSURIOSO
My lords we're pleased to thank you—though we know
'Tis but your duty now to wish it so.
1 NOBLE
That shine makes us all happy. 5
3 NOBLE
His Grace frowns?
2 NOBLE Yet we must say he smiles.
1 NOBLE I think we
must.
LUSSURIOSO
[*Aside*] That foul incontinent duchess we have banished:
The bastard shall not live. After these revels

22 *the other* ed. (the tother Q)
1 s.d. *then enters* [LUSSURIOSO] ed. (*then enters the Duke* Q)

---

s.d. *possessing*. Coronation, installation as duke.
blazing star a stage effect as simple, naive and half-comical as those in Miracle Plays; cf. Samuel Beckett's stage direction "the moon rises at back, mounts the sky, stands still" in Act I of *Waiting for Godot*.

I'll begin strange ones: he and the stepsons
Shall pay their lives for the first subsidies; 10
We must not frown so soon, else 't'ad been now.

1 NOBLE
My gracious lord please you prepare for pleasure;
The mask is not far off.

LUSSURIOSO We are for pleasure:
Beshrew thee what art thou? Madest me start!
Thou hast committed treason!—A blazing star! 15

1 NOBLE
A blazing star! Oh where my lord?

LUSSURIOSO Spy out.

2 NOBLE
See see my lords, a wondrous dreadful one!

LUSSURIOSO
I am not pleased at that ill-knotted fire,
That bushing-flaring star. Am not I duke?
It should not quake me now. Had it appeared 20
Before it, I might then have justly feared:
But yet they say, whom art and learning weds,
When stars wear locks they threaten great men's heads.
Is it so? You are read my lords.

1 NOBLE May it please your Grace,
It shows great anger.

LUSSURIOSO That does not please our Grace. 25

2 NOBLE
Yet here's the comfort my lord: many times
When it seems most, it threatens farthest off.

LUSSURIOSO
Faith and I think so too.

1 NOBLE Beside my lord,
You're gracefully established with the loves
Of all your subjects; and for natural death, 30

21 *Before it* i.e. the coronation
23 *wear locks* bright trails caused by their shooting or falling
23 *wear* ed. (were Q)
27 *most,* Q; Harrier emends to *most near* but Q's meaning is clear enough: "most threatening to you"
farthest ed. (fardest Q)

---

21 *Before it, I* Q; Nicoll emends to *Before, it I* but I see no reason to change Q's meaning "before I became duke".
30–35 The stylisation of the action strongly recalls Middleton's comic method.

I hope it will be threescore years a-coming.

LUSSURIOSO

True—no more but threescore years?

1 NOBLE

Fourscore I hope my lord.

2 NOBLE

And fivescore I.

3 NOBLE

But 'tis my hope my lord you shall ne'er die.

LUSSURIOSO

Give me thy hand: these others I rebuke: 35
He that hopes so, is fittest for a duke.
Thou shalt sit next me. Take your places, lords,
We're ready now for sports, let 'em set on.

[*looks at blazing star*]

You thing! We shall forget you quite anon.

3 NOBLE

I hear 'em coming my lord.

Enter the mask of revengers (*the two brothers* [VINDICE *and* HIPPOLITO] *and two lords more*)

LUSSURIOSO

Ah 'tis well! 40
[*Aside*] Brothers, and bastard, you dance next in hell!

The revengers dance. At the end [*they*] *steal out their swords and these four kill the four at the table, in their chairs. It thunders*

VINDICE

Mark: thunder! Dost know thy cue, thou big-voiced crier?
Duke's groans are thunder's watchwords.

HIPPOLITO

So my lords, you have enough.

VINDICE

Come let's away—no lingering.

HIPPOLITO

Follow—go! 45

Exeunt [*all but* VINDICE]

VINDICE

No power is angry when the lustful die:
When thunder claps, heaven likes the tragedy. *Exit*

LUSSURIOSO

Oh, oh.

42 *big-voiced* ed. (big-voyc'st Q)

---

42 There is close similarity to Hoffman's response to thunder's insistent peals, demanding that he revenge
"againe I come, I come, I come" (*Tragedy of Hoffman* I, i).

Enter the other mask of intended murderers, stepsons [AMBITIOSO *and* SUPERVACUO], *bastard* [SPURIO], *and a fourth man coming in dancing.* [LUSSURIOSO] *recovers a little in voice and groans, calls "A guard! Treason!" at which they all start out of their measure, and turning towards the table they find them all to be murdered*

SPURIO
Whose groan was that?
LUSSURIOSO Treason. A guard.
AMBITIOSO
How now! All murdered!
SUPERVACUO Murdered! 50
4 LORD
And those his nobles?
AMBITIOSO [*Aside*] Here's a labour saved:
I thought to have sped him. 'Sblood—how came this?
[SUPERVACUO]
Then I proclaim myself. Now I am duke.
AMBITIOSO
Thou duke! Brother thou liest. [*stabs* SUPERVACUO]
SPURIO Slave! So dost thou.
[*stabs* AMBITIOSO]
4 LORD
Base villain, hast thou slain my lord and master? 55
[*stabs* SPURIO]

Enter the first men [VINDICE, HIPPOLITO *and two lords*]

VINDICE
Pistols, treason, murder, help, guard! My lord the duke!

[*Enter* ANTONIO *and guard*]

HIPPOLITO
Lay hold upon these traitors! [*guard seizes* 4 LORD]
LUSSURIOSO Oh.
VINDICE
Alas the duke is murdered.

48 s.d. [LUSSURIOSO] ed. (*the Duke* Q)
48 s.d. *measure* dance
53 speech prefix SUPERVACUO ed. (*Spu.* Q)
54 SPURIO ed. (*Spu.* Q)
57 *these traitors!* ed. (this Traytors? Q)

54–55 I have followed previous editors' stage directions which account for the deaths of Supervacuo, Ambitioso and Spurio.

HIPPOLITO And the nobles.

VINDICE
Surgeons, surgeons!— [*Aside*] heart, does he breathe so long?

ANTONIO
A piteous tragedy, able to make 60
An old man's eyes bloodshot.

LUSSURIOSO Oh.

VINDICE
Look to my lord the duke. [*Aside*] A vengeance throttle him!—
Confess thou murderous and unhallowed man,
Didst thou kill all these?

4 LORD None but the bastard, I.

VINDICE
How came the duke slain then?

4 LORD We found him so. 65

LUSSURIOSO
Oh villain.

VINDICE
Hark.

LUSSURIOSO Those in the mask did murder us.

VINDICE
Law! You now sir:
Oh marble impudence—will you confess now?

4 LORD
'Sblood, 'tis all false! 70

ANTONIO
Away with that foul monster
Dipped in a prince's blood.

4 LORD Heart 'tis a lie.

ANTONIO
Let him have bitter execution. [*Exit* 4 LORD *guarded*]

VINDICE
[*Aside*] New marrow! No I cannot be expressed.—
How fares my lord the duke?

LUSSURIOSO Farewell to all: 75
He that climbs highest has the greatest fall.
My tongue is out of office.

VINDICE Air, gentlemen, air.—
[*Whispers*] Now thou'lt not prate on't, 'twas Vindice murdered thee!

60 *make* ed. (wake Q)
63 *unhallowed* ed. (unhollowed Q)
70 *'Sblood* ed. (Sloud Q)

LUSSURIOSO
Oh.

VINDICE
[*Whispers*] Murdered thy father!

LUSSURIOSO Oh.

VINDICE [*Whispers*] And I am he!
Tell nobody.—[LUSSURIOSO *dies*] So, so. The duke's
departed. 80

ANTONIO
It was a deadly hand that wounded him;
The rest, ambitious who should rule and sway
After his death, were so made all away.

VINDICE
My lord was unlikely.

HIPPOLITO Now the hope
Of Italy lies in your reverend years. 85

VINDICE
Your hair will make the silver age again,
When there was fewer, but more honest men.

ANTONIO
The burden's weighty and will press age down:
May I so rule that heaven may keep the crown.

VINDICE
The rape of your good lady has been 'quited 90
With death on death.

ANTONIO Just is the law above.
But of all things it puts me most to wonder
How the old duke came murdered.

VINDICE Oh my lord.

ANTONIO
It was the strangeliest carried: I not heard of the like.

HIPPOLITO
'Twas all done for the best my lord. 95

VINDICE
All for your Grace's good. We may be bold
To speak it now: 'twas somewhat wittily carried
Though we say it. 'Twas we two murdered him!

ANTONIO
You two?

VINDICE
None else i' faith my lord. Nay 'twas well managed. 100

84 *unlikely* unpromising
89 *may* ed. (nay Q)
94 *heard* ed. (hard Q) 96–98 realigned from Q

ANTONIO
Lay hands upon those villains.
VINDICE How? On us?
ANTONIO
Bear 'em to speedy execution.
VINDICE
Heart! Was't not for your good my lord?
ANTONIO
My good! Away with 'em! Such an old man as he!
You that would murder him would murder me! 105
VINDICE
Is't come about?
HIPPOLITO 'Sfoot brother you begun.
VINDICE
May not we set as well as the duke's son?
Thou hast no conscience: are we not revenged?
Is there one enemy left alive amongst those?
'Tis time to die when we are ourselves our foes. 110
When murderers shut deeds close this curse does seal 'em:
If none disclose 'em, they themselves reveal 'em!
This murder might have slept in tongueless brass
But for ourselves, and the world died an ass.
Now I remember too, here was Piato 115
Brought forth a knavish sentence once:
No doubt—said he—but time
Will make the murderer bring forth himself.
'Tis well he died, he was a witch!
And now my lord, since we are in for ever 120
This work was ours, which else might have been slipped;
And if we list we could have nobles clipped
And go for less than beggars. But we hate
To bleed so cowardly: we have enough—

102 *to* ed. (two Q)
111 *murderers* ed. (murders Q)
114 *died* ed. (dyed Q) possibly in the sense of *dye* = "colour, mark deeply"
115–117 realigned from Q
119 *witch* because, evidently, he could prophesy

---

105 Thus Antonio provides an illustration of the general law propounded by Machiavelli:
"He who is the cause of another becoming powerful is ruined; because that predominancy has been brought about either by astuteness or else by force, and both are distrusted by him who has been raised to power"—*The Prince*, trans. W. K. Marriott (London, 1908), ch. III.

I' faith we're well—our mother turned, our sister true, 125
We die after a nest of dukes! Adieu.

Exeunt [VINDICE *and* HIPPOLITO *guarded*]

ANTONIO

How subtly was that murder closed! Bear up
Those tragic bodies; 'tis a heavy season.
Pray heaven their blood may wash away all treason.

[*Exeunt omnes*]

FINIS

127 *closed* disclosed
129 s.d. [*Exeunt omnes*] ed. (*Exit.* Q)